Vaadin 7 UI Design By Example Beginner's Guide

Build exciting Vaadin applications in no time

Alejandro Duarte

BIRMINGHAM - MUMBAI

Vaadin 7 UI Design By Example Beginner's Guide

First published: July 2013

Production Reference: 1190713

Published by Packt Publishing Ltd.
Livery Place
35 Livery Street
Birmingham B3 2PB, UK.

ISBN 978-1-78216-226-1

www.packtpub.com

Cover Image by Jarek Blaminsky (milak6@wp.pl)

Credits

Author

Alejandro Duarte

Reviewers

Martin Cremer

Max Matveev

Henri Muurimaa

Michael Vogt

Acquisition Editor

Martin Bell

Lead Technical Editor

Arun Nadar

Technical Editors

Mrunmayee Patil

Pragati Singh

Hardik B. Soni

Project Coordinator

Shiksha Chaturvedi

Proofreader

Mario Cecere

Indexer

Monica Ajmera Mehta

Graphics

Ronak Dhruv

Production Coordinators

Arvindkumar Gupta

Kirtee Singhan

Cover Work

Arvindkumar Gupta

About the Author

Alejandro Duarte learned how to program at age 13 using the Basic language on a black screen with a blinking cursor. He used to spend hours thinking of ideas for software that would be good to have and even more hours bringing these ideas to life. Alejandro graduated from National University of Colombia with a BS in Computer Science and has been involved in many Java-related software development projects. He first started working with Struts 2 and quickly switched to more RIA friendly frameworks such as Grails, jQuery, GWT, and Vaadin. Alejandro is the author of the Enterprise App for Vaadin add-on and InfoDoc Pro, both open source projects based on the Vaadin framework. He currently works as a developer for several companies and customers mainly in Colombia, Chile, India, Kenya, and the UK.

When not writing code, Alejandro splits his free time between his family, his beautiful girlfriend, and his passion for the electric guitar. You can contact him at `alejandro.d.a@gmail.com` or through his personal blog `http://www.alejandrodu.com`. If you are feeling social, you can follow him on Twitter at `@alejandro_du`.

Acknowledgement

I would like to thank the entire team from Packt Publishing, Ashvini, Martin, Shiksha, and Arun, thanks for trusting me. I thank all the technical reviewers and proofreaders for providing me with valuable feedback from which I have learned a lot. Thanks to Mario Pérez and Camilo Gonzáles from National University of Colombia for introducing me as a professional to the world of software development. Thanks to Colombitrade and all Enterprise App for Vaadin users for their support and confidence. A special thanks to the Vaadin team and community for providing such a terrific framework and knowledge base with tons of articles and useful resources. Hope this book reciprocally contributes back to the community.

I can't thank my parents enough for being so helpful and supportive. I would never have written this book without their constant support and exemplary way of teaching. There's no better teacher than a good parent. A special thanks to my brothers, Juan and Edgar, and my cousins, Marcelo, Camilo, and Jonathan, with whom I took my first steps in programming and created a fictional software development company when we were children, DPA Software. Thanks to my sister for her amusing company while writing this book. Last but not least, thank you Viviana for your encouragement when reaching deadlines and for all those beautiful moments you have gave me.

About the Reviewers

Martin Cremer is working as an architect for a company in the financial sector. His work focuses on maintaining and developing reference architecture for web-based enterprise applications with Vaadin as well as supporting developers in their daily work.

Max Matveev is a software development expert with 12 years of expertise in software development. Originally from Khabarovsk, Russia, he is currently living in Zurich, Switzerland and working for one of the largest Swiss banks as the Technical Lead.

With main focus on Enterprise Java, he is experienced in all areas of enterprise software development ranging from backend data processing to modern rich UI web applications.

Always looking for the best user experience possible he is one of those who allowed Vaadin to become one of the bank's standard frameworks for building UI.

In addition to his main work, Max is also author of some popular (with over one million downloads) indie iOS applications. Data processing requirements for the huge user base allowed him to become one of the main pre-production tester of Jelastic SaaS platform during the platform's beta period.

Michael Vogt started in 2000 at Apple, Germany as a WebObjects developer. Since then, he worked in many different companies and countries, mostly as a freelancer on GWT projects. Currently he works in the services department of Vaadin.

www.PacktPub.com

Support files, eBooks, discount offers and more

You might want to visit www.PacktPub.com for support files and downloads related to your book.

Did you know that Packt offers eBook versions of every book published, with PDF and ePub files available? You can upgrade to the eBook version at www.PacktPub.com and as a print book customer, you are entitled to a discount on the eBook copy. Get in touch with us at service@packtpub.com for more details.

At www.PacktPub.com, you can also read a collection of free technical articles, sign up for a range of free newsletters and receive exclusive discounts and offers on Packt books and eBooks.

http://PacktLib.PacktPub.com

Do you need instant solutions to your IT questions? PacktLib is Packt's online digital book library. Here, you can access, read and search across Packt's entire library of books.

Why Subscribe?

- Fully searchable across every book published by Packt
- Copy and paste, print and bookmark content
- On demand and accessible via web browser

Free Access for Packt account holders

If you have an account with Packt at www.PacktPub.com, you can use this to access PacktLib today and view nine entirely free books. Simply use your login credentials for immediate access.

Table of Contents

Preface

Vaadin is an open source framework to ease development of Java web applications that provides a programming model close to Swing or AWT. Vaadin is licensed under the Apache License, is well documented, comes with out-of-the-box theming facilities, and is supported by a committed company and a vibrant community contributing to the framework through forums and hundreds of add-ons.

Vaadin allows developers to write web applications using only Java. Of course, HTML, CSS, and JavaScript are building blocks of web application development, however, by using Vaadin, developers will be maintaining Java code most of the time. The UI layer is implemented using the object-oriented paradigm. This allows developers to bring all the object-oriented knowledge out there directly to their UI layers. Developers missing the joy of using Swing or AWT to build desktop applications when creating web applications usually love Vaadin.

This book will teach you how to develop Java web applications in minutes. Starting from chapter one, you will begin with simple examples and quickly move towards more complex applications covering UI components, themes, custom components, and client-side applications.

What this book covers

Chapter 1, Writing Your First Vaadin-powered Application, explains how to set up your development environment and create your first Vaadin project.

Chapter 2, Using Input Components and Forms – Time to Listen to Users, explains basic usage of input components and the Vaadin data model.

Chapter 3, Arranging Components into Layouts, covers layout components, panels, pop-up windows, tab sheets, and accordions.

Chapter 4, *Using Vaadin Navigation Capabilities*, deals with using Vaadin to build more website-like applications.

Chapter 5, *Using Tables – Time to Talk to Users*, covers one of the most useful and powerful UI components in Vaadin: the table component.

Chapter 6, *Adding More Components*, introduces several UI components such as trees, progress indicators, icons, sliders, color pickers, images, web content, and drag and drop.

Chapter 7, *Customizing UI Components – Time to Theme it*, covers Vaadin theme creation using CSS and Sass.

Chapter 8, *Developing Your Own Components*, introduces the strategies to develop pure client-side applications and custom components.

What you need for this book

To run the examples and follow the tutorials in this book, you will need Java SDK installed. You will need also Eclipse, NetBeans, or Maven.

Who this book is for

This book is ideal for developers with a good knowledge of Java willing to build rich-Internet applications using Vaadin. Basic understanding of HTML and CSS is useful but not required to understand the content of the book.

Conventions

In this book, you will find several headings appearing frequently.

To give clear instructions of how to complete a procedure or task, we use:

Time for action – heading

1. Action 1
2. Action 2
3. Action 3

Instructions often need some extra explanation so that they make sense, so they are followed with:

What just happened?

This heading explains the working of tasks or instructions that you have just completed.

You will also find some other learning aids in the book, including:

Pop quiz – heading

These are short multiple-choice questions intended to help you test your own understanding.

Have a go hero – heading

These practical challenges give you ideas for experimenting with what you have learned.

You will also find a number of styles of text that distinguish between different kinds of information. Here are some examples of these styles, and an explanation of their meaning.

Code words in text, database table names, folder names, filenames, file extensions, pathnames, dummy URLs, user input, and Twitter handles are shown as follows: "Change your code to add the required text fields before creating the button instance."

A block of code is set as follows:

```
new Button.ClickListener() {
  public void buttonClick(ClickEvent event) {
    // this will be called if button is clicked
  }
}
```

When we wish to draw your attention to a particular part of a code block, the relevant lines or items are set in bold:

```
public class WelcomeUI extends UI {

  protected void init(VaadinRequest request) {
    VerticalLayout layout = new VerticalLayout();
    setContent(layout);

    Button button = new Button("Click Me");
    layout.addComponent(button);
  }

}
```

Any command-line input or output is written as follows:

```
mvn archetype:generate -DarchetypeGroupId=com.vaadin -
DarchetypeArtifactId=vaadin-archetype-application -
DarchetypeVersion=7.0.0 -Dpackaging=war
```

New terms and **important words** are shown in bold. Words that you see on the screen, in menus or dialog boxes for example, appear in the text like this: "You can right-click on your project and select **Debug As | Run Jetty**."

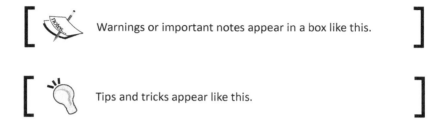

> Warnings or important notes appear in a box like this.

> Tips and tricks appear like this.

Reader feedback

Feedback from our readers is always welcome. Let us know what you think about this book—what you liked or may have disliked. Reader feedback is important for us to develop titles that you really get the most out of.

To send us general feedback, simply send an e-mail to feedback@packtpub.com, and mention the book title via the subject of your message.

If there is a topic that you have expertise in and you are interested in either writing or contributing to a book, see our author guide on www.packtpub.com/authors.

Customer support

Now that you are the proud owner of a Packt book, we have a number of things to help you to get the most from your purchase.

Downloading the example code

You can download the example code files for all Packt books you have purchased from your account at http://www.packtpub.com. If you purchased this book elsewhere, you can visit http://www.packtpub.com/support and register to have the files e-mailed directly to you.

Errata

Although we have taken every care to ensure the accuracy of our content, mistakes do happen. If you find a mistake in one of our books—maybe a mistake in the text or the code—we would be grateful if you would report this to us. By doing so, you can save other readers from frustration and help us improve subsequent versions of this book. If you find any errata, please report them by visiting http://www.packtpub.com/submit-errata, selecting your book, clicking on the **errata submission form** link, and entering the details of your errata. Once your errata are verified, your submission will be accepted and the errata will be uploaded on our website, or added to any list of existing errata, under the Errata section of that title. Any existing errata can be viewed by selecting your title from http://www.packtpub.com/support.

Piracy

Piracy of copyright material on the Internet is an ongoing problem across all media. At Packt, we take the protection of our copyright and licenses very seriously. If you come across any illegal copies of our works, in any form, on the Internet, please provide us with the location address or website name immediately so that we can pursue a remedy.

Please contact us at copyright@packtpub.com with a link to the suspected pirated material.

We appreciate your help in protecting our authors, and our ability to bring you valuable content.

Questions

You can contact us at questions@packtpub.com if you are having a problem with any aspect of the book, and we will do our best to address it.

1
Writing Your First Vaadin-powered Application

So you want to start creating cool web applications in Java? Well, you've come to the right place. Vaadin is a mature, powerful Java framework to build modern web applications leveraging your Java programming skills, and understanding of concepts such as listeners, components, and other well-known constructions acquired from the desktop APIs such as Swing and AWT.

First things first. Downloading, installing, and configuring your development environment are the first steps to get started with Vaadin. In this chapter we will cover the following topics:

- Creating and running Vaadin applications in Eclipse
- Creating and running Vaadin applications in NetBeans
- Creating and running Vaadin applications using Maven
- Generated application explained
- Buttons
- Labels
- Text fields
- Notifications

We will cover the details of configuring your development environment using Eclipse, NetBeans, and Maven. Feel free to jump straight to the section explaining your favorite IDE and skip those covering the other ones.

Let's get our hands dirty!

Creating and running Vaadin applications in Eclipse

If you are using NetBeans, another IDE, or no IDE at all, you can safely skip this section.

Installing Eclipse

Just in case you haven't already done so, you will need to download and install Eclipse, the preferred IDE for developing Vaadin applications.

Time for action – downloading and installing Eclipse

Steps to download and install Eclipse are as follows:

1. Go to `http://eclipse.org/` and download the latest (or your favorite) version of Eclipse for Java EE Developers.
2. Extract the downloaded file to the directory you would like Eclipse to be installed in.
3. Execute `eclipse.exe` or `eclipse` according to your operating system flavor.

What just happened?

Guess what? We've just downloaded and installed Eclipse. Seriously, that was the very first step; now we need to install the Vaadin plugin for Eclipse.

Installing the Vaadin plugin for Eclipse

In this section we will see how to install the Vaadin plugin for Eclipse.

Time for action – installing the plugin

Steps to install the Vaadin plugin for Eclipse are as follows:

1. In Eclipse, go to **Help | Eclipse Marketplace...**.
2. Type `Vaadin` in the **Find** field inside the **Search** tab and press *Enter*.

3. Click on the **Install** button besides the **Vaadin Plugin for Eclipse** heading.

4. Eclipse will calculate some requirements and dependencies. Once it does, make sure the **Vaadin Plugin for Eclipse** is checked and click on **Next**.

5. Read and accept the terms of the license agreement and click on **Finish** to start installing the plugin.

> I always keep processes like this running in the background. This helps me to be more productive because I can read or write some code, change configuration, deploy to a server, or perform any other IDE related action while having the background process moving forward.

6. The installation process can take some minutes. You will be prompted to accept installing software that contains unsigned content. Click on **OK** when asked to and let Eclipse continue with the installation.

7. Finally, Eclipse will ask you if you want to restart the IDE. Do it. Once you restart Eclipse, you'll see a little reindeer logo on the toolbar, that's the Vaadin logo and means that the plugin is ready.

What just happened?

We've just prepared Eclipse to start hacking! Using the Vaadin Plugin for Eclipse we'll be able to create new Vaadin projects, custom components, and themes. But before that, we will have to install a web server to deploy our Vaadin applications.

> You might have noted that the Vaadin Plugin for Eclipse installed an additional plugin: **IvyDE**. Ivy is a tool for managing dependencies, usually all the JAR files that your project needs. Don't worry too much if you don't know Ivy, just go through the following steps and we will get some fun in a couple of minutes, I promise.

Installing Run Jetty Run plugin

Although we can deploy to most Java servers, we will use Jetty throughout this book. Jetty is a fast open source web server that implements the *Java Servlet* and *JavaServer Pages* technologies. These technologies make it possible to develop web applications using Java.

Time for action – installing Jetty

Steps to make Eclipse a Jetty-ready IDE are as follows:

1. Go to **Help | Eclipse Marketplace...** in Eclipse.
2. Type `Run Jetty Run` in the **Find** field inside the **Search** tab and press *Enter*.
3. Click on the **Install** button besides the Run Jetty Run plugin.
4. Make sure **Run Jetty Run** is checked and click on **Next**.
5. Accept the license agreement and click on **Finish**.
6. The installation process can take some minutes. You will be prompted to accept installing software that contains unsigned content. Click on **OK** when asked to and let Eclipse continue with the installation.
7. Once Eclipse finishes installing the plugin, it will ask you if you want to restart the IDE. Do it again.

What just happened?

We've successfully downloaded and installed our own Jetty server.

Now we are ready to create and deploy our first Vaadin-powered application.

Creating a new Vaadin project in Eclipse

The Vaadin plugin for Eclipse includes a wizard to easily create new Vaadin projects.

Time for action – creating a new Vaadin project

Steps to create a Vaadin application are as follows:

1. Navigate to **File | New | Other....**

2. Go to the **Vaadin** sub tree and select **Vaadin 7 Project**.

3. Click on **Next**.

4. Type `welcome` for your project name and select the latest Vaadin version.

> At the time of writing this book, the latest available version was 7.0.0.

5. Click on **Finish** to let Eclipse create the project for us.

What just happened?

A new project has been created and we can deploy it to our server right away, so let's do it now!

Deploying and running Vaadin applications in Eclipse

Till now we have seen how to create a project, now we will see how to deploy and run the project. We are ready to see our application up and running.

Time for action – deploying and running

Steps to deploy and run a Vaadin application are as follows:

1. Click on the **Debug As...** button on the toolbar and go to **Debug As | Run Jetty**.

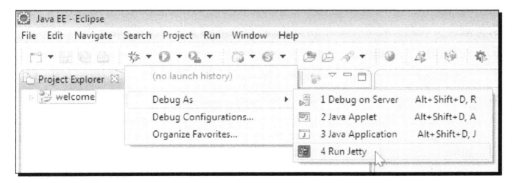

2. Alternatively, you can right click on your project and select **Debug As | Run Jetty**.

3. Using your preferred browser, go to `http://localhost:8080/welcome` and play with the just created Vaadin application.

What just happened?

We have created, deployed, and run a Vaadin application using Eclipse. Upcoming applications will be generated way faster because we won't need to install any more plugins.

Creating and running Vaadin applications in NetBeans

You can completely skip this section if you don't want to use NetBeans to develop Vaadin applications. Stay tuned otherwise.

Installing NetBeans

NetBeans is an open source IDE similar to Eclipse, which allows developers to create web applications using Java.

Time for action – downloading and installing NetBeans

Installing NetBeans is quite easy. Let's see how it's done.

1. Go to the URL `http://netbeans.org/` and download the latest (or your favorite) version of NetBeans Java EE edition.

2. Run the just downloaded installation file.

3. The installation program will allow you to choose whether to install Apache Tomcat or Glassfish. Although you can use most Java servers, we will use Tomcat to deploy our applications. So, make sure you check Apache Tomcat and click on **Next**.

4. Accept the terms of the license agreement and click on **Next**.

5. Accept the terms of the JUnit license agreement and click on **Next**.

6. Select the directory you would like NetBeans to be installed to and click on **Next**.

7. Select the directory you would like Tomcat to be installed to and click on **Next**.

8. Click on **Install** to start the installation process.

9. Once the installation process is finished, you will be prompted to contribute to the NetBeans project. If you wish to, check the corresponding option and click on **Finish**, otherwise just click on the **Finish** button.

What just happened?

As you can guess, we have installed NetBeans and we are ready to create our first Vaadin project.

Creating a new Vaadin project in NetBeans

The best and the easiest way to create Vaadin 7 projects in NetBeans is by using Maven. Fortunately, NetBeans have very good support for Maven projects. If you don't know Maven, don't worry, be happy (thanks Bobby). Follow these steps and you'll get a Vaadin application willing to be hacked right away.

Time for action – creating a new Vaadin project

Steps to create a new Vaadin project are as follows:

1. Go to **File** | **New Project...** and select **Project from Archetype** under the **Maven** category. Click on **Next**.

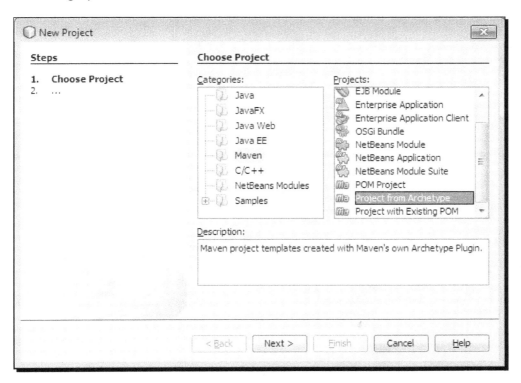

2. Type `vaadin` in the **Search** field and select **vaadin-archetype-application**.
Click on **Next**.

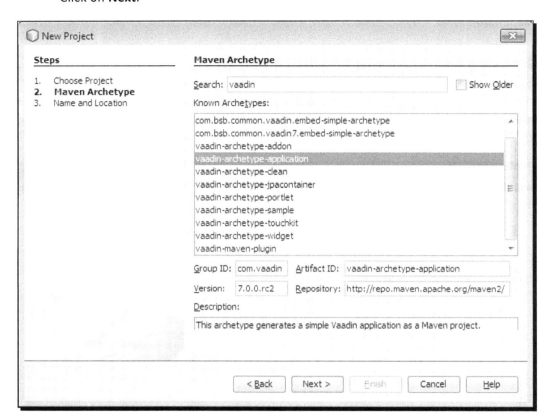

 You can think of Maven archetypes as project wizards maintained online.
Maven will take care of all JARs needed.

3. Enter `welcome` as **Project name** and click on **Finish**.

 You may want to fill in the rest of the fields with your preferred values,
but for this first application, defaults are just fine.

What just happened?

A new project has been created and we can deploy it to our server right away, so let's
do it now!

Deploying and running Vaadin applications in NetBeans

We are ready to see our application up and running.

Time for action – deploying and testing

Steps for deploying and testing the Vaadin application in NetBeans are as follows:

1. Deploying an application in NetBeans couldn't be easier. Just select your welcome project and click on that little green arrow on the toolbar:

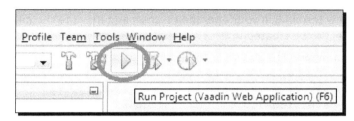

2. Alternatively, you can do the same using the menu **Run | Run Project (Vaadin Web Application)**. Even faster: *F6*.

3. NetBeans will prompt you to select a server. You've installed Tomcat, right? Select the Apache Tomcat server and click on **OK**. Note that you can deploy to any server you have registered in NetBeans, we are using Tomcat just for the purposes of this example.

4. Once you select the server, you will see a lot of messages on the output console. This is Maven preparing your application. Be patient, this process could take a while, only the first time.

5. Go to `http://localhost:8084/welcome` and play with the just created Vaadin application.

What just happened?

We have successfully created, deployed, and run a Vaadin application using NetBeans.

Creating and running Vaadin applications using Maven

You can completely skip this section if you don't want to use Maven to develop Vaadin applications. If you want to, and you are using NetBeans, please read the previous section if you haven't already.

Vaadin 7 Maven archetype

You are still here. Chances are that you are not using Eclipse or NetBeans. Well, actually, the easier way to get Vaadin 7 is through Maven. We are not covering how to install Maven here. If you haven't already, install Maven following the instructions given in `http://maven.apache.org`.

Time for action – creating a new Vaadin project

Steps for creating a new Vaadin project are as follows:

1. Open a new terminal in your operating system and move to the directory you want your project to be created in.

2. Run the command line shown as follows:

   ```
   mvn archetype:generate -DarchetypeGroupId=com.vaadin -
   DarchetypeArtifactId=vaadin-archetype-application -
   DarchetypeVersion=7.0.0 -Dpackaging=war
   ```

3. Enter your preferred **groupId** and press *Enter*. For example, `com.example.welcome`.

4. Enter `welcome` as **artifactId** and press *Enter*.

5. Press *Enter* to accept the default version.

6. Press *Enter* to accept the default package.

7. Confirm that everything is OK by typing `Y` and press *Enter*.

What just happened?

If you can see the rewarding **BUILD SUCCESS** message, you have successfully created your first Vaadin project using Maven. You must have a new directory with all the generated files for your project.

Deploying and running Vaadin applications with Maven

Deploying to Jetty is so common that we just can't break the old tradition of using it to test our application.

Time for action – deploying and running

Steps for deploying and running Vaadin applications with Maven are as follows:

1. Move to the directory that Maven created for your project. If you have specified `welcome` as **artifactId**, then move to the `welcome` directory.

2. Before actually deploying the application we must compile it and package it. To do that, run the command:

   ```
   mvn package
   ```

3. This will take some time, so be patient.

4. Now we are ready. Run the command:

   ```
   mvn jetty:run
   ```

5. If you haven't run this before, you will see a very verbose Maven downloading stuff.

    Just in case if you want to break the old tradition:
   ```
   mvn tomcat:run
   ```

6. Go to `http://localhost:8080/welcome` and play with the just created Vaadin application.

What just happened?

We have successfully created, compiled, packaged, deployed, and run a Vaadin application using Maven.

Generated application explained

We have completed the first step of configuring our development environment to develop and run Vaadin applications. Now let's get started with the real cool stuff: the code.

Open the file `WelcomeUI.java` (or `MyVaadinUI.java` if you are using NetBeans or Maven). You will see something like this:

```
package com.example.welcome;

import com.vaadin.server.VaadinRequest;
import com.vaadin.ui.Button;
import com.vaadin.ui.Button.ClickEvent;
import com.vaadin.ui.Label;
import com.vaadin.ui.UI;
```

```
import com.vaadin.ui.VerticalLayout;

public class WelcomeUI extends UI {

  protected void init(VaadinRequest request) {
    final VerticalLayout layout = new VerticalLayout();
    layout.setMargin(true);
    setContent(layout);

    Button button = new Button("Click Me");
    button.addClickListener(new Button.ClickListener() {
      public void buttonClick(ClickEvent event) {
        layout.addComponent(new Label("Thank you for clicking"));
      }
    });
    layout.addComponent(button);
  }
}
```

This is going to be like a crash course on Vaadin 7. Let's pretend that we have created the previous class starting with an empty one like the following (package and import declarations will be omitted):

```
public class WelcomeUI {
}
```

This class will be the root of all our UI components. When you create a Vaadin application, and once the user browses to the URL the application has been deployed to, a web page will be automatically generated using the logic you've implemented in a certain method of this class. Which method? One overridden from the UI class, so first, we got to extend the UI class as follows:

```
public class WelcomeUI extends UI {
}
```

And the method to override is as follows:

```
public class WelcomeUI extends UI {

  protected void init(VaadinRequest request) {
  }

}
```

Where is the `init` method called from? A Java web application is implemented using the **Servlet** technology. In short, a `Servlet` is a class that adds functionality to a web server. You can pair URLs with your own `Servlet` implementations and call any code you need to fulfill the requirements for your application. You do this in the `web.xml` file (or using annotations). Vaadin has a custom `Servlet` implementation which can be configured to call your own UI class implementation. Take a look at the `web.xml` file and find the Vaadin Servlet (`com.vaadin.server.VaadinServlet`).

Because this method will be called when the user browses to the application URL, you have the chance to build the user interface here. This is done by building a components tree. It's like a hierarchy where the components are arranged. We have already created the root component for the hierarchy, our `WelcomeUI` class. Now we can add visual components into the root component. But let's first see graphically how the component hierarchy should look when we finish our piece work:

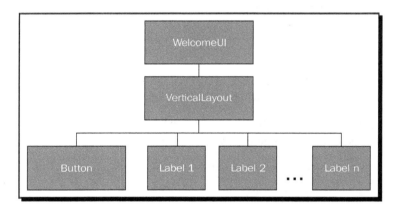

What we have here is a **WelcomeUI** having a **VerticalLayout** which has a **Button** and some **Labels**. VerticalLayout, what's that? Think of it as an invisible component that allows you to arrange its child components vertically on the page, one upon another. So the button is on the top, then goes the first label, then the second label, and so forth.

Ok, back to the code. Take a look at how we can add that `VerticalLayout` invisible thing:

```
public class WelcomeUI extends UI {

  protected void init(VaadinRequest request) {
    VerticalLayout layout = new VerticalLayout();
    setContent(layout);
  }

}
```

We've created an instance of `VerticalLayout` and then set it to be the content of the UI. By calling the `setContent(layout)` method we are saying that `layout` is a child of our `WelcomeUI` instance.

Buttons

Now we have a layout in which we can add the button and all the *n* labels. Let's do it for the button:

```
public class WelcomeUI extends UI {

  protected void init(VaadinRequest request) {
    VerticalLayout layout = new VerticalLayout();
    setContent(layout);

    Button button = new Button("Click Me");
    layout.addComponent(button);
  }

}
```

No rocket science. We create an instance of `Button` and add it to the `layout`. This means the `button` is a child of `layout`, it will be displayed inside the `VerticalLayout`.

At this point, if we run the application, a button will be shown but it won't produce any response when clicked. Let's change that boredom:

```
public class WelcomeUI extends UI {

  protected void init(VaadinRequest request) {
    VerticalLayout layout = new VerticalLayout();
    setContent(layout);

    Button button = new Button("Click Me");
    button.addClickListener(new Button.ClickListener() {
      public void buttonClick(ClickEvent event) {
        // this will be called when button is clicked
      }
    });
    layout.addComponent(button);
  }

}
```

Don't be afraid, we've added five lines of code, but most of them are brackets or comments. `Button` has a method that allows you to add click listeners. A click listener is a class that listens to click events, that's it. Here, we are using an anonymous class (you know Java, right?):

```
new Button.ClickListener() {
  public void buttonClick(ClickEvent event) {
    // this will be called if button is clicked
  }
}
```

This class is an anonymous implementation of the `Button.ClickListener` interface. We are passing the just created instance to the `addClickListener` method in order to connect our code with the click event on the button. This kind of usage of anonymous classes is very common when developing Vaadin applications, especially in places where you need this callback behavior.

Labels

We are ready to add the logic needed to dynamically add all those labels into the layout. We have a listener defining a method that will be called each time the button is clicked. So let's add the corresponding logic in that method:

```
public class WelcomeUI extends UI {

  protected void init(VaadinRequest request) {
    final VerticalLayout layout = new VerticalLayout();
    setContent(layout);

    Button button = new Button("Click Me");
    button.addClickListener(new Button.ClickListener() {
      public void buttonClick(ClickEvent event) {
        Label label = new Label("Thank you for clicking");
        layout.addComponent(label);
      }
    });
    layout.addComponent(button);
  }

}
```

This is similar to when we added a button to the layout. This time we're adding a label. A label allows you to show non-editable texts.

Have a go hero – display some HTML text

`Label` components can display text in several formats. You can display plain text (that's the default), preformatted text, and HTML text. What if you want to display the "Thank you" part of the message on the label using a bold font?

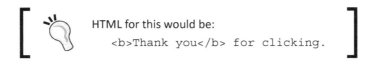

HTML for this would be:
```
<b>Thank you</b> for clicking.
```

You are one line far of doing that. Try it! Use the `setContentMode` method of `Label` and the `ContentMode` enumeration to display HTML messages on your page.

Layout margin

If we run the application right now, we will see a screen as shown in the following screenshot (before clicking the button several times, of course):

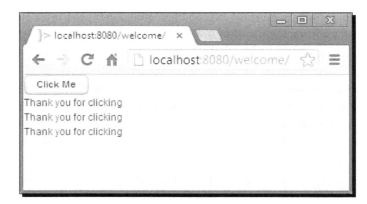

It looks a little tight on the page. We can add some space around the `layout` using the `setMargin` method as shown in the following code snippet:

```java
public class WelcomeUI extends UI {

  protected void init(VaadinRequest request) {
    final VerticalLayout layout = new VerticalLayout();
    layout.setMargin(true);
    setContent(layout);

    Button button = new Button("Click Me");
    button.addClickListener(new Button.ClickListener() {
      public void buttonClick(ClickEvent event) {
```

```
        Label label = new Label("Thank you for clicking");
        layout.addComponent(label);
      }
    });
    layout.addComponent(button);
  }


}
```

Now it will appear as follows:

That's it. If you make some little refactor, you will get the original application that your IDE (or Maven) created.

A more interesting "hello world" application

Now that you understand the code of the generated application, let's try adding a couple of features to make it a little bit more interesting. First, that boring "Thank you" message is not very useful. What if we develop an application that generates some random funny phrases? The user enters the name of two friends or something, and the application will produce random phrases about them.

Text fields

Text fields are the components we need to allow the user to enter the two names. Do you remember how we added the **Click Me** button? Adding text fields is the same story.

Time for action – using text fields

Follow these steps to add some fun to our application:

1. Change your code to add the required text fields just before the line that creates the `button` instance by adding the highlighted code:

```
// ...
setContent(layout);

final TextField name1 = new TextField("Somebody's name");
final TextField name2 = new TextField("somebody's name");
layout.addComponent(name1);
layout.addComponent(name2);

Button button = new Button("Click Me");
// ...
```

2. Add the business logic in a new method like this:

```
public String getFunnyPhrase(String name1, String name2) {
  String[] verbs = new String[] {
    "eats", "melts", "breaks", "washes", "sells"};

  String[] bodyParts = new String[] {
    "head", "hands", "waist", "eyes", "elbows"};

  return name1 + " " +
    verbs[(int) (Math.random() * 100 % verbs.length)] + " " +
    name2 + "'s " +
    bodyParts[(int) (Math.random() * 100 % verbs.length)];
}
```

3. Change the listener to display the message returned by the business method:

```
public void buttonClick(ClickEvent event) {
  String phrase = getFunnyPhrase(
      name1.getValue(), name2.getValue());
  layout.addComponent(new Label(phrase));
}
```

What just happened?

We added a couple of text fields to our layout and then implemented a method to get the message to be shown on the labels. As you may have already guessed, the TextField class defines a getValue() method which returns the value which the user has introduced in the field. In this case, it happens to be a String. All input components (that is, components that get input from a user) have a getValue() method, which we can use to know the values introduced on the user interface. The following is a screenshot of the application (it seems that Maria doesn't like Juan too much):

Notifications

Notifications are a common feature in applications. You might need to notify that some event has occurred in your system when the user performs certain action. For example, in a **CRUD** (create, read, update, and delete) interface, your application should notify the user whether each action has been successfully executed or not.

Vaadin makes it easy for you to show fancy notifications in your web applications. The Notification class has several static methods you can call from any part of your code to show notifications. For simple notifications you can make a call such as:

```
Notification.show("User created");
```

This will display a message centered on the page shown as follows:

The message will disappear when the user moves the mouse or presses any key.

Have a go hero – show notifications

In the funny phrases application, it would be nice if the application alerts the user when no names are given instead of showing no-sense phrases. Would you be able to modify the application in order to make it show this alert using the Notification class? Try it!

Downloading the example code

You can download the example code files for all Packt books you have purchased from your account at http://www.packtpub.com. If you purchased this book elsewhere, you can visit http://www.packtpub.com/support and register to have the files e-mailed directly to you.

Pop quiz – Vaadin fundamentals

There are a couple of concepts you must keep in mind to be proficient with Vaadin. Answer the following questions and test yourself about your current Vaadin level.

Q1. Which method will be automatically called when somebody browses to your application URL?

1. UI.setContent(Component component).
2. UI.init(VaadinRequest request).
3. VerticalLayout.init(VaadinRequest request).
4. VerticalLayout.addComponent(Component component).

Q2. Suppose you are overriding the init method of your own UI class. How would you set the root of your components tree?

1. By calling the setContent method of the UI class and passing the root component.

2. By calling the addComponent method of the UI class and passing the root component.

3. Actually, an instance of the UI class I'm writing will be the root of the tree.

4. There's no such a thing as a components tree (it seems the book's author is going crazy).

Summary

We learned some cool features in this chapter:

◆ We configured our development environment using Eclipse, NetBeans, and Maven.

◆ We learned the details of the code IDE wizards (or Maven) generated when we create a new project.

◆ We learned how components are internally arranged in a tree, where the root is a class extending UI.

◆ We learned that the init method of our UI class is like a starting point for building our user interface.

◆ We used labels and buttons and attached them to a vertical layout.

◆ We also learned how easy it is to show notifications using the static methods of the Notification class.

Now you are able to develop simple web applications using Vaadin. The next chapter will teach you how to use more complex input components.

2
Using Input Components and Forms –
Time to Listen to Users

You must be feeling eager to get more of Vaadin. What if we take a look at some of the input components Vaadin has to offer? In this chapter, we will take a closer look at the main components for retrieving and processing all the data that users want your application to be aware of. Read this chapter and you will be able to develop a lot of new useful rich Internet applications using Vaadin.

This chapter will cover the following topics:

- Separating business classes from UI classes
- Responding to value changes in input components
- Getting and setting the value of input components
- Tooltips and error indicators
- Underlying Vaadin technologies
- UI components hierarchy
- Vaadin's data model
- Comboboxes, checkboxes, text areas, option groups, twin column selects, and date/time pickers
- File uploading

It's time to have some fun. Keep reading.

The Time It application

A couple of years ago I was working with some friends on a personal Java project. We used to meet every Saturday to review what we had done before building the entire system. Let me introduce you to my friends: Susan Obstinate and Mark Nowsitall (weird last names, aren't they?).

"I've spent the entire week writing this code, but it's ready now," said Susan with an embittered tone.

"Let me see how you handled that," replied Mark suspiciously. Though they didn't seem to be, they were a couple.

So Susan proudly showed us her piece of code:

```
// some nasty code was here (censored for respect of the reader)
public String getUglyUrl(long total) {
    String url = "http://localhost/app/someservice?code=";

    for(long i = 0; i < total; i++) {
        url += someTrickyMath(i);
    }

    return url;
}

public String someTrickyMath(long i) {
    // (censored)
}
```

"We can use an `int` object type instead of `long` for the loop in your `getUglyUrl` method," instantly affirmed Mark.

"I don't think we need that," said Susan.

"You could also use a `StringBuilder` class to..." I started to say, but suddenly got interrupted by Mark.

"An `int` object type would improve performance a lot. The `int` comparisons and manipulations are faster than `long` ones," Mark explained.

"What if the total gets too big? We'd need a `long` object type then," Susan argued.

"Total has never gone beyond 10,000 and I highly doubt it will in the near future," Mark replied.

We (actually it was Mark) finally managed to convince Susan to change her code.

There are lots of situations similar to this one, more complicated, and with tons of external factors that make it hard to be 100 percent sure about which of two code strategies will work faster. Let's take advantage of this story and develop a nice Vaadin application for timing code.

Note: please read the following sentence using a flamboyant and jazzy voice.

Introducing: *Time It!* The application that will show some facts to Susan.

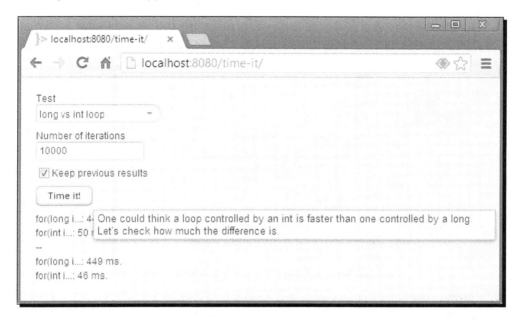

Time for action – separating business classes from UI classes

Vaadin is mostly about UI. Vaadin's motto *thinking of U and I* is not in vain. I said mostly because you can additionally find a bunch of useful add-ons to deal with server-side technologies. Even Vaadin itself ships with some data components.

 There are lots of integration add-ons for Vaadin. For instance, you can integrate with technologies such as Groovy, Spring Framework, SQL, JPA, Hibernate, Lucene, Google App Engine Datastore, Quartz, JasperReports, JFreeChart, OpenLayers, Google Maps, OpenID, and even Twitter! All this with one hand tied behind your back. Visit https://vaadin.com/directory.

Most, if not all, applications have some kind of business logic. That is, something to do with the application's data. If you are an experienced developer you will agree with me that separating business logic from UI logic makes a lot of sense. For the "Time It" application, we will use two Java packages to separate business logic from UI logic:

1. Create a new Vaadin project named *time-it* using your IDE.

2. Delete the all the generated classes. We will add our own classes in a minute.

3. Create the following package. Don't worry about the classes right now. Just create the Java packages `timeit`, `timeit.biz`, `timeit.biz.test`, and `timeit.ui`:

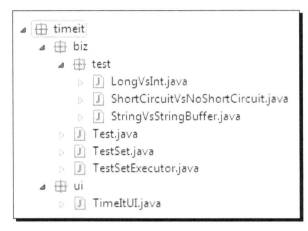

4. Browse the book's source code and copy all the classes inside the `biz` package and paste them into your own `biz` package. Don't copy `TimeItUI.java`, we will work on that through the chapter.

5. Create a new class with the `TimeItUI` name inside the `ui` package.

6. Update your `web.xml` file to use `TimeItUI` as the starting application:

```xml
<servlet>
  <servlet-name>Time It</servlet-name>
  <servlet-class>com.vaadin.server.VaadinServlet</servlet-class>
  <init-param>
    <description>
    Vaadin UI class to use</description>
    <param-name>UI</param-name>
      <param-value>timeit.ui.TimeItUI</param-value>
  </init-param>
</servlet>
<servlet-mapping>
  <servlet-name>Time It</servlet-name>
  <url-pattern>/*</url-pattern>
</servlet-mapping>
```

7. Let's start with an outline of our `TimeItUI` class. Modify your `TimeItUI` class to match something like this:

```
public class TimeItUI extends UI {

    ... some variables ...

    @Override
    protected void init(VaadinRequest request) { ... }

    private void initCombo() { ... }

    private void initButton() { ... }

    private void initLayout() { ... }

    public boolean validate() { ... }

    public void runSelectedTest() { ... }

    private void showResults(Collection<String> results) { ... }

}
```

What just happened?

Of course, the `TimeItUI` class won't compile. But now you have an outline with the structure of methods we will implement through the chapter. Just keep reading.

Most of the application is about business (the `biz` package) with only one class handling our UI logic. However, we will focus on the UI part. Business classes are not puzzling at all. We will use them as black boxes in our `TimeItUI` class (that's the reason we are just copying them).

 I've faced several situations where I needed to modify UI components calling lots of business methods on classes that were completely unknown to me. Sometimes, I only had access to remote EJBs' interfaces code, there was no way to look at the actual implementation. When modifying UI layers, treat business logic as black boxes and use unit testing to prevent introducing regression bugs.

UI components as class members

In the example of the previous chapter, we created UI components as they were needed inside methods. This time, for the "Time It" application, we will declare most of the UI components as class members.

Time for action – adding components as class members

To add UI components as class members, edit your `TimeItUI` class by adding these variables to it:

```
private static final TestSet[] testSets = new TestSet[] {
  new LongVsInt(),
  new StringVsStringBuffer(),
  new ShortCircuitVsNoShortCircuit()
};

private VerticalLayout layout = new VerticalLayout();
private ComboBox combo = new ComboBox("Test");
private final TextField textField = new TextField("Number of
                                    iterations", "1000");
private CheckBox checkBox = new CheckBox("Keep previous results");
private Button button = new Button("Time it!");
private VerticalLayout resultsLayout = new VerticalLayout();
```

What just happened?

The first thing you see, `testSets`, is just an array of business objects, specifically, an array containing instances of `TestSet` (take a look at the `TestSet` interface in the book's source code). Think of `TestSet` as a single scenario from which we want to obtain timing results. For example, the `LongVsInt` class will run two tests: one to time a loop controlled by a `long` object type and another to time a loop controlled by an `int` object type. If you want to add some testing scenarios, all you must do is to implement the `TestSet` interface and add a new instance to the `testSets` array.

Time for action – adding some infrastructure

Edit the `init` method of your `TimeItUI` class to match the following:

```
@Override
protected void init(VaadinRequest request) {
  initCombo();
  initButton();
  initLayout();
}
```

What just happened?

Here we are breaking up the functionality to initialize our UI components in a more suitable way by implementing smaller methods. Now that we have the required infrastructure, we can start adding input components.

Comboboxes

A combobox is an input component that allows users to select an option from a drop-down list. It looks like the following screenshot:

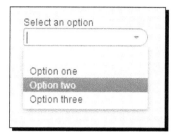

You must be thinking "yeah right, but how do you put those options in there?" This is easy:

```
ComboBox c = new ComboBox("Select an option");
c.addItem("Option one");
c.addItem("Option two");
c.addItem("Option three");
```

If you have the options in a Java Collection class, you can pass the Collection instance to the constructor like this:

```
ArrayList<String> options = new ArrayList<>();
options.add("Option 1");
options.add("Option 2");
options.add("Option 3");
ComboBox c = new ComboBox("Select an option", options);
```

The method addItem accepts an Object, so we can pass instances of any class. For example, if we had a User class we could have done this:

```
User user1 = new User("Jurka", "Rahikkala");
User user2 = new User("Joonas", "Lehtinen");

ComboBox c = new ComboBox("Select a user");
c.addItem(user1);
c.addItem(user2);
```

Now, how will the ComboBox component know what to print as option captions? First, let's go back to our "Time It" application.

Time for action – adding a combobox

Implement the `initCombo` method of your `TimeItUI` class as shown in the following code snippet:

```
private void initCombo() {
  for(TestSet testSet : testSets) {
    combo.addItem(testSet);
    combo.setItemCaption(testSet, testSet.getTitle());
  }

  combo.addValueChangeListener(new ValueChangeListener() {
    @Override
    public void valueChange(ValueChangeEvent event) {
      TestSet testSet = (TestSet) combo.getValue();
      textField.setValue("" + testSet.getDefaultTimes());
      button.setDescription(testSet.getDescription());
    }
  });

  combo.setImmediate(true);
}
```

What just happened?

It's not that complicated. If we isolate the `for` portion of the previous code, we'll get this:

```
for(TestSet testSet : testSets) {
  combo.addItem(testSet);
  combo.setItemCaption(testSet, testSet.getTitle());
}
```

For each `TestSet` instance in our array, we add a `TestSet` instance and then we say, "Okay, Vaadin for this `testSet` array I just added, please show what `testSet.getTitle()` returns. Thank you very much". We are adding instances of `TestSet` and explicitly specifying what we want to be shown for each option inside the `ComboBox` component.

> If we don't specify an item caption, Vaadin will call `testSet.toString()` and use the returned value as caption. That's the default behavior, but you can use the `setItemCaptionMode` method to specify different strategies to get the caption for each item in a `ComboBox` instance. If you are curious, take a look at the API documentation for `ComboBox` at `https://vaadin.com/api/`.

Responding to value changes

So, we have our `combo` ready and showing all available tests. If you have already played with the application, you may have noted that when you select a test, the number of iterations shown in the text field and the button tooltip explaining the test are updated accordingly. Well, the rest of the `initCombo` method implements this functionality.

Do you remember when we added a `ClickListener` instance for the button in the previous chapter? We are doing something similar here. This time, we are adding a `ValueChangeListener` instance to execute our code when the user selects an option:

```
combo.addValueChangeListener(new ValueChangeListener() {
  @Override
  public void valueChange(ValueChangeEvent event) {
    // your code here
  }
});
```

Getting and setting the value of input components

The user selects one option, the `valueChange` method of our anonymous listener is called, and now we can update the value in `textField`. That's one line of code:

```
textField.setValue(theValue);
```

Wait... how do we know what is the selected value in the combobox? If `setValue` is for setting the value, then `getValue` is for getting the value! Unbelievable! Let's get the value:

```
TestSet testSet = (TestSet) combo.getValue();
```

Now that we have the value, we can easily set the text in the `textField`:

```
textField.setValue("" + testSet.getDefaultTimes());
```

We've just learned something valuable (it's not wordplay): input components, they all have the `getValue` and `setValue` methods.

Tooltips

A tooltip is boxed text that appears when the user holds the mouse pointer over a UI element. The following screenshot shows a Vaadin tooltip:

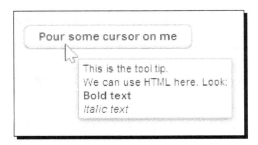

Adding tooltips is a piece of cake. All we need to do is the following:

```
button.setDescription(testSet.getDescription());
```

Most UI components include this method. You can put any HTML you want to nicely format your tooltips.

Immediate mode

There is just one final line that we have not explained yet in the initCombo method:

```
combo.setImmediate(true);
```

This makes the component respond as soon as the user changes its value (and after the component loses focus). If we don't put this line, when the user changes the value, Vaadin could say "Okay, I will wait for some more events before I send that change in combo". This is not only for the ComboBox component, all input components have this method too.

> When you are developing Vaadin applications, you may get to a point where you have a listener for a component but the listener is not getting called when expected. Check that you have activated the immediate mode in your component.

Error indicators

We must provide feedback to the user when the input is incorrect. Error indicators are a way to provide such feedback.

Time for action – validating user input

We can run a `TestSet` instance only if the user selects one. Follow these steps to add a proper validation:

1. Implement your `initButton` method to match this code:

```
private void initButton() {
  button.addClickListener(new ClickListener() {
    @Override
    public void buttonClick(ClickEvent event) {
      if(isValid()) {
        runSelectedTest();
      }
    }
  });
}
```

2. Now implement your `validate` method. Here is how we validate:

```
public boolean isValid() {
  combo.setComponentError(null);
  textField.setComponentError(null);

  boolean isValid = true;

  if(combo.getValue() == null) {
    combo.setComponentError(
        new UserError("Select a test from the list."));
    isValid = false;
  }

  if(textField.getValue().toString().isEmpty()) {
    textField.setComponentError(new UserError(
        "You must introduce the number of iterations to execute"));

    isValid = false;
  }

  return isValid;
}
```

What just happened?

For the button listener, it's the same as in previous chapter. We have a button and we want to respond to click events, so we add `ClickListener`, using an anonymous class.

As you can see, if the `isValid` method returns `true`, we proceed to run the selected test. First two lines of the method are for clearing any error we may have added to the components in previous executions of the `isValid` method itself. Then, we declare a flag that will tell us whether the components have valid values or not. If the selected value in `combo` is null, we add an error message to the component using the following code line:

```
combo.setComponentError(new UserError("Select a test from the
    list."));
```

`setComponentError` expects an instance of `ErrorMessage`. `UserError` is an implementation of the `ErrorMessage` interface that allows us to show an error message on the component. Usually, the component will show an error indicator. If the user places the mouse cursor over the component, a tooltip will appear showing the error text:

A similar logic is used to show an error over `textField` if the users left it empty.

Vaadin comes with three flavors of errors, `UserError`, `SystemError`, and `CompositeErrorMessage`, as follows:

- `UserError` is an error that we, programmers, generate as a result of validations
- `SystemError` is used where there is a problem in the system (for example, an uncaught exception)
- `CompositeErrorMessage` allows you to show multiple error messages

Layout spacing

We have our components ready. We know how they respond to events (clicks and value changes) and how they communicate. We still have to know how the tests are executed and how the results are shown. But first, let's incorporate all those components into the main layout.

Time for action – adding input component into the layout

Implement your `initLayout` method using the following snippet of code:

```
private void initLayout() {
    layout.setMargin(true);
    layout.setSpacing(true);
    layout.addComponent(combo);
    layout.addComponent(textField);
    layout.addComponent(checkBox);
    layout.addComponent(button);
    layout.addComponent(resultsLayout);

    setContent(layout);
}
```

What just happened?

We let the layout to have an appropriate margin and spacing. This last one adds some space between components instead of having them bonded inside the layout. Following that, we add `combo`, `textField`, `checkBox`, `button`, and a `VerticalLayout` component to put some labels for showing the results of the test case execution. Finally, the last statement sets layout as content of the page.

Checkboxes

Everyone knows checkboxes. Have you ever accepted license agreements during software installations? Just in case, this is a checkbox:

☐ Check me if you know check boxes

We have already created our checkbox:

```
private CheckBox checkBox = new CheckBox("Keep previous results");
```

 The `getValue` and `setValue` methods of `CheckBox` return `Boolean` objects, no need to cast the returned value as we did with the `combo` component. You can do just this:

```
Boolean checked = checkBox.getValue();
```

Removing components from layouts

Before explaining how we show the results, let's see how we can execute the selected `TestSet` instance.

Time for action – running the test set

Implement your `runSelectedTest` method. This method will be called when the user presses the **Time it!** button:

```
public void runSelectedTest() {
  Long times = Long.parseLong(textField.getValue());
  Collection<String> results = TestSetExecutor.execute(
      (TestSet) combo.getValue(), times);
  showResults(results);
}
```

What just happened?

Here, we're converting the string stored in the text field to a `Long` number using `Long.parseLong` (a potential exception, `NumberFormatException`, pokes its head).

Once we have the `Long` value, we execute the results using a helper class in the `biz` package (`TestSetExecutor`). This helper class has an `execute` method that expects the `TestSet` to execute and the number of iterations to perform for each test in the `TestSet`. The `execute` method returns all the results as a collection of strings that we can proudly show to the user. As proudly as Susan when she presented her code.

Have a go hero – add a validation to Time It

When converting the value in `textField`, the method `parseLong` will throw an evil `NumberFormatException` if the string to parse is not a number. Try it! Use "Time It" and type a wrong numeric expression in the text field. Now try making "Time It" a production-ready application by adding the missing validation (inside the `isValid` method) to show a proper error message when incorrect input is given for the `textField` component.

Time for action – showing the results

The default behavior of the application is to show only the results of the last execution. We need to remove all the results that have been previously added to the `resultsLayout` component if the user has not checked **Keep previous results**. To do that, implement your `showResults` method:

```
private void showResults(Collection<String> results) {
  if(!checkBox.getValue()) {
```

```
        resultsLayout.removeAllComponents();

    } else if(resultsLayout.getComponentCount() > 0) {
      resultsLayout.addComponent(new Label("--"));
    }

    for(String result : results) {
      resultsLayout.addComponent(new Label(result));
    }
  }
```

What just happened?

If the checkbox is not checked, we can remove all the components in `resultsLayout` (not in `layout`, we don't want baffled users here):

```
resultsLayout.removeAllComponents();
```

If we don't have to remove previous results, we add a separator and iterate over the results to add each one using a label.

 You can remove single components from layouts using the `removeComponent` method:

```
layout.removeComponent(someComponent);
```

Congratulations! We have finished a useful application. Try implementing your own test sets and learn more about Java performance.

Thinking in Vaadin

Your brain must have started to feel comfortable using UI components such as labels, text fields, comboboxes, buttons, vertical layouts, and notifications. You know how to respond to events on these components by implementing click listeners and value change listeners. You can get the introduced (or selected) values from input components, and you can wire all this up inside a custom class extending Vaadin's `UI`.

The rest of the trip in this book is about learning more components, how to respond to events on components, and how to make them look as we want them to look. To prepare your brain for this trip, we will right now cover some basic theory about Vaadin. So relax, close your IDE for a little while, and let your fingers have a rest while we learn some nuts and bolts of Vaadin.

Servlets and GWT

How can Vaadin render all those nice widgets on the browser using only an instance of a class (the one that extends `UI`)? Let's expose Vaadin's magic.

We can easily think of the browser making requests to a web server. In fact, the first thing we do when we are using a Vaadin application is to request a URL, something like `http://localhost:8080/webapp`. When we do this, the server will respond with an HTML page that the browser is able to render. The server (or web container in the Java ecosystem) is a software component that understands HTTP operation quite well. What the server doesn't understand well are our particular requirements, so the server just delegates that part to other components. We create these components, and we do it by using a powerful Java technology called **servlet**.

`Servlet` is a class that processes requests and constructs responses. We map URLs with the `Servlet` classes in a web deployment descriptor (`web.xml`). For example:

```
<servlet>
  <servlet-name>My servlet</servlet-name>
  <servlet-class>my.package.MyVeryOwnServlet</servlet-class>
</servlet>
<servlet-mapping>
  <servlet-name>My servlet</servlet-name>
  <url-pattern>/myurl/*</url-pattern>
</servlet-mapping>
```

With this configuration, an instance of `my.package.MyVeryOwnServlet` will be created and invoked when a URL such as `http://localhost:8080/webapp/myurl` is requested. We are not covering the details of **Servlet** technology here, just make sure you understand that the `MyVeryOwnServlet` class will generate a response (probably an HTML response) when the mapped URL is invoked. This response contains the HTML that the browser will render as depicted in the following figure:

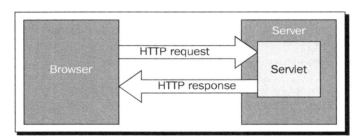

Well, it turns out that Vaadin comes with a `Servlet` implementation, `com.vaadin.server.VaadinServlet`. We use this ready-to-use `Servlet` class to create Vaadin applications. `VaadinServlet` will handle all the HTTP requests for us. That's nice, but, how the heck can `VaadinServlet` construct an HTML response showing all our UI components? When you configure `VaadinServlet` in your `web.xml` file (actually the IDE does it for us when we create a new Vaadin project), you must give the fully qualified name of your `UI` class as a parameter of the servlet, as shown in the following code snippet:

```
<init-param>
    <description>Vaadin UI class to use</description>
    <param-name>UI</param-name>
    <param-value>my.package.MyUI</param-value>
</init-param>
```

This goes inside the `<servlet>` tag in `web.xml`. Here we are connecting our logic with the ready-to-use servlet, `VaadinServlet`. Now, it is able to create an instance of our `UI` class and start working to generate the HTML response for us based on the components tree that we have constructed:

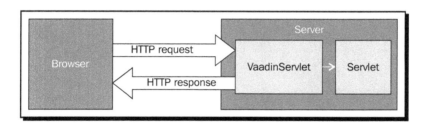

It seems to be that `VaadinServlet` has a lot of work to do now. Well, it certainly has, but `VaadinServlet` takes advantage of another cool technology: **Google Web Toolkit** (or GWT for short). It is a set of open source tools to develop web applications based on HTML and JavaScript.

Web application development is basically the process of creating applications that are to be shown on a web browser. The browser understands HTML and JavaScript, so we ultimately have to generate HTML and JavaScript to build web user interfaces. This means that most of the time you must be proficient enough with HTML, JavaScript, and the backend programming language (probably Java). When a new developer joins your team, you must be sure that the new guy knows these languages well, right? Not at all if you are using GWT (and Vaadin of course!).

GWT, and therefore Vaadin, are capable of converting your Java UI classes into equivalent JavaScript. Actually, what GWT does is to compile your Java code and generate JavaScript that communicates with your server-side components. By using GWT solely you are using a client-side technology. GWT takes your classes and compiles them to JavaScript. You still need to handle all the communication happening between the client and the server, so you will end up with some classes being compiled to JavaScript and some classes handling the communication and server-side logic. Vaadin hides the complexity of developing this communication logic by providing an API on top of GWT, while still allowing you write pure client-side applications. Vaadin is like an augmented version of GWT.

Back to the servlet part, `VaadinServlet` takes advantage of GWT to generate JavaScript and HTML while adding all the client/server communication plumbing for you. This will lead to simpler architectures in your applications.

UI components hierarchy

UI components form an interesting hierarchy. Take a look at the main interfaces and abstract classes in the hierarchy:

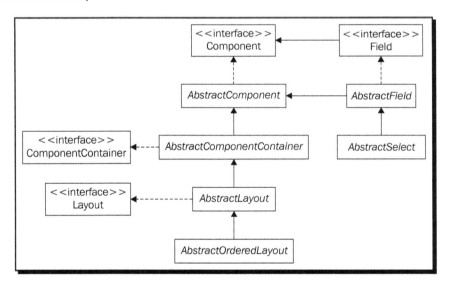

Component

The Component interface is the root of the hierarchy, which means that you can assign any UI component to a Component reference. We have already used a method declared in this interface, the setDescription method (to display tooltips). This class also declares methods (usually getters and setters) to deal with common properties of UI components. The following table shows some of these properties:

Property	Methods in Component	Description
Enabled	isEnabled() setEnabled(boolean)	If enabled, the user cannot interact with the component. I'm disabled :(I'm enabled :D
Caption	getCaption() setCaption(String)	The caption is the text that allows the user to know the component intention. Most of the time we give the caption using a constructor. This is the caption
Visible	isVisible() setVisible(boolean)	Visible components are shown, invisible component are not.
Read only	isReadOnly() setReadOnly(boolean)	Users cannot change the value of read only components.
Icon	getIcon() setIcon(Resource)	An icon is an image accompanying the component. ✓ Ok
Parent	getParent()	Returns the parent component in the components tree.

The following is the list of components seen in the previous figure:

◆ `AbstractComponent` provides a default implementation for all the methods in the `Component` interface, plus some methods to handle size, errors, and immediate mode.

◆ The `ComponentContainer` interface defines common methods to add and remove components to other components.

◆ The `AbstractComponentContainer` class extends `AbstractComponent` and defines the default implementation for all the methods in `ComponentConainer`. So, an `AbstractContainer` interface is `AbstractComponent`, and of course, you can use it as a `Component`. Additionally, you can add and remove components to it.

◆ `Layout` is an extension of `ComponentContainer` that defines inner interfaces to handle alignment, spacing, and margin.

◆ The `AbstractLayout` class extends `AbstractComponentContainer` and defines the default implementation for all the methods in `Layout`.

◆ The `AbstractOrderedLayout` class is the base class for layouts that need to keep components in linear order. `VerticalLayout` extends this class.

◆ The `Field` interface is the base interface for input components.

◆ The `AbstractField` class extends `AbstractComponent` and provides basic functionality for input components. `TextField` and `Button` are the examples of the classes extending `AbstractField`.

◆ `AbstractSelect` is a base class for input components that allows users to select items. `ComboBox` is the component of an `AbstractSelect` class.

Vaadin's data model

UI components can manage data using a simple yet powerful generic data model. This model is an abstraction that allows UI components to be bound to several data sources, such as filesystems or databases.

 Data binding is the process of establishing a connection between UI components and data sources. If the data changes then UI components act accordingly.

The data model is a central topic when developing Vaadin applications. It provides a framework for implementing any representation of the underlying data. This means that it's possible to represent (or display) any kind of data, from filesystems to database queries. Vaadin has a number of ready-to-use implementations of the data model and they are used as the default data model for many of the input components.

The model breaks up the data in three main concepts: **properties**, **items**, and **containers**. In short, a container has many items and an item has many properties.

Well, we have been talking too seriously for too many paragraphs; it's time to have some fun.

Time for action – binding data to properties

There's no better way to learn than practice. Follow these steps to see how binding works in real life:

1. Create a new project named *binding* using your IDE. A Vaadin one, of course.

2. Don't hesitate and delete all the content in the generated `BindingUI` class.

3. Create a new local instance of `TextField` and turn immediate mode on:

    ```
    @Override
    protected void init(VaadinRequest request) {
      TextField textField = new TextField("Data");
      textField.setImmediate(true);
    }
    ```

4. Create a new local instance of `Label`:

    ```
    Label label = new Label();
    ```

5. Add the `TextField` and `Label` components to a new `VerticalLayout` and set it to be the content of the UI:

    ```
    VerticalLayout layout = new VerticalLayout();
    layout.addComponent(textField);
    layout.addComponent(label);
    setContent(layout);
    ```

6. Nothing new so far, so create a new instance of the `ObjectProperty` class:

    ```
    ObjectProperty<String> property =
                    new ObjectProperty<String>("the value");
    ```

7. Wow, that was new. More newness, bind the property to the UI components:

    ```
    textField.setPropertyDataSource(property);
    label.setPropertyDataSource(property);
    ```

8. Deploy and run the application. Try changing the value in the `textField` component. While testing the application, make sure you click out of the `textField` or press *Tab* after changing its value, so the change will be sent to the server.

What just happened?

We bound two UI components to a single data source. One of the components (TextField) is capable of changing the data source (ObjectProperty) while the other just displays the data in the data source. Here is a screenshot:

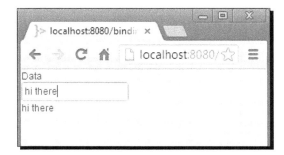

If you change the value in the TextField component, it will in turn change the data source, causing the Label component to display the new value. textField and label are both connected to the same data source via the ObjectProperty instance:

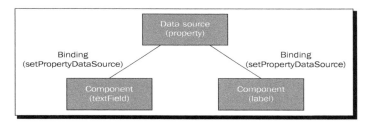

This is useful because we can easily attach a single data source to multiple views (UI components).

What is property anyway? It is an object containing a value of a certain type. In the previous example, the type was String. The Property class is an interface, and Vaadin provides several implementations for this interface. We are using the ObjectProperty implementation that allows us to wrap any Java object into a property.

The `Property` interface has some methods to get and set the value, to get and set the read only state, and to get the type of the stored value. This is a graphical depiction of a property:

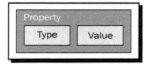

Items

Items are a way to group properties. Before grouping the properties each one receives an ID, the property ID (or PID):

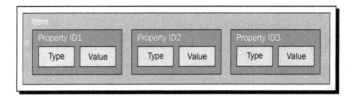

Think of a Java object. It has several properties each one with its own name. For example:

```
class User {
    String login = "bill";
    String password = "pass";
    Boolean enabled = true;
}
```

We can model this data abstraction using properties and items:

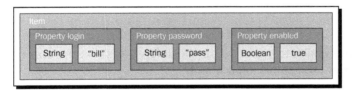

Items are used in components that deal with more complex data than labels or text fields. For example, Vaadin includes a `FormGroup` class that can be bound to an item.

Containers

Last, but not least, a **container** is a way to group items. And again, before grouping the items, each one receives an ID, the item ID (or IID):

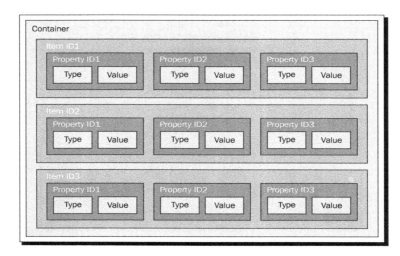

Two common Vaadin components that can be bound to containers are `Table` and `Tree`.

More input components

It's time to continue with our trip. Vaadin has several built-in input components (or fields as they implement directly or indirectly the `Field` interface). All these components extend from `AbstractField` or `AbstractSelect`. Let's take a look at some of them.

Text area

`TextArea` is quite similar to `TextField`. The difference is that the user can enter multiline texts. Take a look at this sample application:

```java
public class TextareaUI extends UI implements ValueChangeListener {

    @Override
    protected void init(VaadinRequest request) {
        // our TextArea component
        TextArea textArea = new TextArea(
            "Enter some multi-lined text and press TAB:");
        textArea.addValueChangeListener(this);
        textArea.setImmediate(true);

        VerticalLayout layout = new VerticalLayout();
```

```
      layout.addComponent(textArea);
      setContent(layout);
   }

   @Override
   public void valueChange(ValueChangeEvent event) {
      String userText = event.getProperty().getValue()
         .toString();
      Notification.show("This is it: " + userText);
   }

}
```

That's easy. It's the same as using `TextField`. We create an instance and add it to some layout. We are not using an anonymous class for `ValueChangeListener` this time. We let `TextAreaUI` implement `ValueChangeListener` and define the corresponding `valueChange` method.

Have a go hero – disable word wrap

By default, `TextArea` will word wrap the text in the field. However, you can disable this by using the `setWordwrap` method. Try it! Call this method giving `false` as parameter and test the application typing a long word like `honorificabilitudinitatibus`.

Rich text area

A `RichTextArea` component allows complex styling and formatting. Take a look at the example application:

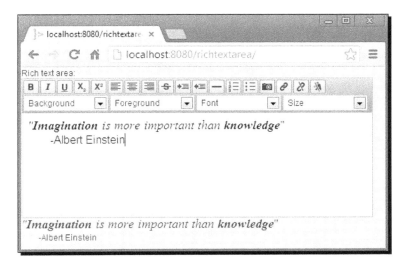

Here is what goes in the `init` method:

```
RichTextArea richText = new RichTextArea("Rich text area:");
richText.setImmediate(true);
Label label = new Label(richText, ContentMode.HTML);

VerticalLayout layout = new VerticalLayout();
layout.addComponent(richText);
layout.addComponent(label);
setContent(layout);
```

Pretty straightforward except for the `Label` constructor. The constructor we are calling is this:

```
public Label(Property contentSource, ContentMode contentMode)
```

Is `RichTextArea` a `Property`? That makes no sense! In fact it makes a lot of sense. A `Field` interface stores a typed value, and `Property` is just that. Remember we saw that `AbstractField` is the default implementation of the `Field` interface? Well, `Field` itself extends `Property`. So any `Field` is a `Property` too.

> The `RichTextArea` component stores the value as a `String` containing HTML (or more precisely, XHTML). A user could try to attempt a **cross-site scripting** attack here. This kind of attack is about injecting malicious JavaScript code that could be executed later. If you think that a user can input HTML that another user could see, parse the HTML so you can be sure no offensive JavaScript could be executed. This process is also known as **sanitizing**.

Option groups

`OptionGroup` is an alternative to `ComboBox`, it allows the user to select elements. The usage is similar to `ComboBox`:

```
OptionGroup og = new OptionGroup(
    "Are you enjoying the book?");
og.addItem("Oh yeah");
og.addItem("Kind of");
og.addItem("Not really");
```

This is how the previous `OptionGroup` code would be rendered:

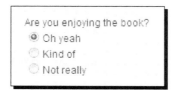

Hope you agree with the answer in the screenshot. You can easily disable individual options. For example, to disable the **Kind of** option, we can use this line of code:

```
og.setItemEnabled("Kind of", false);
```

If you want to use HTML on the options, use this code:

```
og.setHtmlContentAllowed(true);
```

Now take a look at this example:

```
public class OptiongroupUI extends UI implements
    ValueChangeListener {

  @Override
  protected void init(VaadinRequest request) {
    // an array with the options
    ArrayList<String> answers = new ArrayList<String>();
    answers.add("Vaadin beans");
    answers.add("Session beans");
    answers.add("Enterprise App for Vaadin beans");
    answers.add("Message-driven beans");

    // our OptionGroup component
    OptionGroup og = new OptionGroup(
        "Two kinds of EJBs in Java EE are:", answers);
    og.addValueChangeListener(this);
    og.setImmediate(true);

    // our main layout
    VerticalLayout layout = new VerticalLayout();
    layout.addComponent(og);
    setContent(layout);
  }

  @Override
  public void valueChange(ValueChangeEvent event) {
    String answer = event.getProperty().getValue().toString();
    Notification.show("Your answer: " + answer);
  }

}
```

Note that we are getting the value in `OptionGroup` through the event variable that allows us to get the property bound to the field that triggered the value change event.

This application has a fundamental problem. We are asking the user to select two options, but the `OptionGroup` component allows only one option to be selected at a time.

Time for action – fixing the OptionGroup example

It's time for our good deed of the day. `OptionGroup` has a very simple method to turn on a multiple selection mode: `setMultiSelect`.

1. Open or import the *optiongroup* example in your IDE.

2. Add `og.setMultiSelect(true)` after instantiating `og`.

3. Deploy and run the example.

What just happened?

Take a look at the new interface:

As you can see, now the component is displayed as an assortment of checkboxes and the getValue method (of both OptionGroup and Property) returns a Java Collection (actually a Set). This happens when we activate multiselect mode.

 We are not talking about Java EE, but just in case, the correct answers are:

Session beans and **Message-driven beans**

Have a go hero – improve the OptionGroup example

Try changing the OptionGroup example application to show a message informing whether the answer is correct or not. Here is a quick hint: cast the value to a Java Set instance.

Twin column selects

Instead of the OptionGroup component we can use TwinColSelect. We can change OptionGroup for TwinColSelect in the previous example:

```
TwinColSelect og = new TwinColSelect(
        "Two kinds of EJBs in Java EE are:", answers);
```

With this, we get an interesting component for selection:

Date/time pickers

Vaadin includes a nice date/time picker with multiple configuration options. You can add a date picker using this:

```
DateField dateField = new DateField("Select a date");
```

This will display a field to directly type the date and a button to open a convenient calendar:

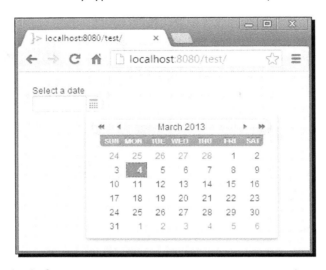

The `getValue` method of `DateField` returns a `java.util.Date` object. You can configure the resolution of `DateField`. For example, to allow users select only a year, we can do this:

```
dateField.setResolution(Resolution.YEAR);
```

This will show a more restrictive component:

Resolution is a Java enum that includes the YEAR, MONTH, DAY, HOUR, MINUTE, and SECOND values to use in your date pickers.

A date format can be specified using the setDateFormat method:

```
dateField.setDateFormat("yyyy-MM-dd");
```

 yyyy-MM-dd is the date format for the ISO 8601 standard.

 If you want to display the entire calendar selector (instead of the input field with the button to open a calendar) use InlineDateField.

Time for action – using an InlineDateField component

Let's change the DateField example a little bit:

1. Open or import the *datefield* example in your IDE.
2. Replace DateField with InlineDateField in DateFieldUI.java.
3. Deploy and run the example.

What just happened?

This is the result you get:

You cannot type the year now, you have to select it from the component.

Uploading files

Study this simple example that displays (in the console) the content of a text file uploaded by the user:

```java
public class UploadUI extends UI implements Receiver {
  @Override
  protected void init(VaadinRequest request) {
    Upload upload = new Upload(
        "Select a text file and look at the console",
        this);

    VerticalLayout layout = new VerticalLayout();
    layout.addComponent(upload);
    setContent(layout);
  }

  @Override
  public OutputStream receiveUpload(String filename,
      String mimeType) {
    return new OutputStream() {
      @Override
      public void write(int b) throws IOException {
        System.out.print((char) b);
      }
    };
  }

}
```

The Upload class displays a native (browser-dependent) button to select a file and a Vaadin button to upload the file to the server:

We are passing a `Receiver` interface (implemented in our `UploadUI` class) to process the upload byte-by-byte. The `receiveUpload` method must return an `OutputStream` class that writes the content of the file being uploaded. In this example, we are taking each byte and printing it on the console, but you can do with the bytes whatever you want to. For example, you could write them to a file in the hard disk or in a BLOB in an SQL database.

No, really, how can we actually write the file to the server? OK, OK, here is a possible implementation of `recieveUpload` that does the job:

```
@Override
public OutputStream receiveUpload(String filename,
    String mimeType) {
  FileOutputStream output = null;

  try {
    output = new FileOutputStream("C:\\Users\\Alejandro\\"
        + filename);
  } catch (FileNotFoundException e) {
    e.printStackTrace();
  }
  return output;
}
```

Pop quiz – thinking in Vaadin

Check your knowledge:

Q1. Which method allows you to add options in a `ComboBox`?

1. `addOption(String option)`.
2. `addItem(String itemId)`.
3. `addItem(Object itemId)`.

Q2. If you want to execute some code when the user changes the value in a `Field` component you must add a:

1. `ValueChangeListener`.
2. `ClickListener`.
3. `ValueChangeEvent`.

Q3. To add a tooltip, you use the method:

1. `setTooltip(String text)`.

2. `addTooltip(String text)`.

3. `setDescription(String text)`.

Q4. You can add an error message to a `Component` by calling:

1. `setErrorMessage(String error)`.

2. `setComponentError(ErrorMessage errorMessage)`.

Q5. All input components implement (directly or indirectly):

1. `Field`.

2. `Property`.

3. All of the above.

Q6. A `Property` is:

1. A value of a certain type.

2. A collection of items.

Summary

This was a big chapter. Look at what we have covered:

- ◆ We learned how to create Vaadin applications that communicate with business classes.

- ◆ We took a look at the underlying technologies that make it possible to write web applications entirely in Java.

- ◆ We got to know the Vaadin data model and its core concepts: properties, items, and containers.

- ◆ We saw a simplified version of the UI components hierarchy.

- ◆ We learned the common functionality for UI components and we saw that this functionality is defined in the `Component` interface paired with the `AbstractComponent` class.

- ◆ We have learned how to use most of the input components available in Vaadin.

So far, our applications have had a boring layout (`VerticalLayout`). In the next chapter we will start making more appealing applications by learning a lot about layouts in Vaadin. See you there.

3
Arranging Components into Layouts

In this chapter, we will learn how to arrange components into layouts. So far, we have been using vertical layouts to place our components. However, Vaadin provides several layout components to fit our needs. In order to learn most layout capabilities in Vaadin, we will develop a small framework to easily build appealing menu-based web interfaces.

This chapter will cover the following topics:

- ◆ Horizontal layouts
- ◆ Components size
- ◆ Expanding components
- ◆ Split panels
- ◆ Changing layouts dynamically
- ◆ Grid layouts
- ◆ Absolute layouts
- ◆ Click listeners
- ◆ Form layouts
- ◆ Panels
- ◆ Tab sheets
- ◆ Accordions
- ◆ Windows

Warm up your fingers and launch your IDE. We are coding a lot here!

Horizontal layouts

There are two types of components in Vaadin: Layout components and non-layout components. We can put both, layout and non-layout components, into layout components. We have already used a layout component, `VerticalLayout`, which allowed us to arrange components in a vertical fashion. What we want to do in this chapter is to build a user interface with a more sophisticated design, something like this:

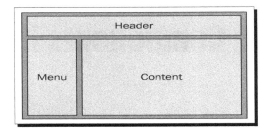

You can think of this design as a big vertical layout containing an upper section and a lower section. The upper section contains only the header while the lower section contains a menu and a content area. These last components on the lower section are arranged not vertically but horizontally.

Time for action – the main layout

Let's start by coding the main layout using our well known friend `VerticalLayout` and the new guy `HorizontalLayout`:

1. Create a new Vaadin project. For this example, we will use *layout-framework* as project name and `LayoutFrameworkUI` as the UI class.

2. Create a new Java class `MainLayout`.

3. Let `MainLayout` extend `VerticalLayout`:

    ```
    public class MainLayout extends VerticalLayout {

    }
    ```

4. Add layouts for upper and lower sections of `MainLayout`:

    ```
    public class MainLayout extends VerticalLayout {

        private VerticalLayout upperSection = new VerticalLayout();
        private HorizontalLayout lowerSection = new
          HorizontalLayout();
        private VerticalLayout menuLayout = new VerticalLayout();
        private VerticalLayout contentLayout = new VerticalLayout();

    }
    ```

5. Add the following default constructor for `MainLayout`:

```
public MainLayout() {
  upperSection.addComponent(new Label("Header"));
  menuSection.addComponent(new Label("Menu"));
  contentSection.addComponent(new Label("Content"));

  lowerSection.addComponent(menuLayout);
  upperSection.addComponent(contentLayout);

  addComponent(upperSection);
  addComponent(lowerSection);
}
```

6. Change the `init` method in your `LayoutFrameworkUI` class to match this:

```
public class LayoutFrameworkUI extends UI {

  protected void init(VaadinRequest request) {
    setContent(new MainLayout());
  }

}
```

7. Compile, deploy, and run your application.

What just happened?

Let's get real; the application doesn't look very impressive so far:

We have created our very own layout class taking advantage of VerticalLayout. So our MainLayout is a VerticalLayout too, but now it contains a VerticalLayout for the header or upper section and a HorizontalLayout for the lower section which in turn contains a menu layout and a content layout, both using VerticalLayout. Layout, layout, layout, what a tongue-twister!

We have added some labels to see how our layout works.

 Note that when we add components into a HorizontalLayout they are placed from left to right.

Take a look at the components tree for MainLayout (we are showing only layout components):

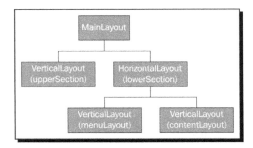

Components size

It seems that the layouts are not the size we want them to be. Or are they? Here is a quick and dirty tip to visualize borders on components.

Time for action – visualizing borders

Follow these steps to visualize borders around components:

1. Add the following method to your MainLayout class:

```
private void showBorders() {
  String style = "v-ddwrapper-over";
  setStyleName(style);
  upperSection.setStyleName(style);
  lowerSection.setStyleName(style);
  menuLayout.setStyleName(style);
  contentLayout.setStyleName(style);
}
```

2. Call the method at the end of the constructor:

```
public MainLayout() {

   . . .

   showBorders();
}
```

3. Run the application and say oh!

What just happened?

We have added a built-in CSS class to the layouts (v-ddwrapper-over). The application now looks like this:

 The setStyleName method allows adding a CSS class to a component. Vaadin has built-in CSS classes that we can use or we can create our own ones. We will cover this interesting topic in *Chapter 7, Customizing UI Components – Time to Theme it.*

Our suspicious were true. The layouts are not the size we need. We want our MainLayout to be like a full screen component occupying all the space on the navigator's page. Actually MainLayout seems to be OK regarding the width. Not the same for the height. We want it to be full size vertically too, that means a 100 percent height for it. On the other hand, lowerSection component seems to be OK regarding the height but not the width.

Adjusting the size for a component is easy. All you need to do is use setWidth and setHeight methods:

```
someComponent.setHeight("100%");
someComponent.setWidth("50%");
someOtherComponent.setWidth("320px");
```

You can specify the size in percentage, pixels, or any other CSS unit.

 There is a shortcut for setting both, width and height, to 100 percent size:

```
component.setSizeFull();
```

Time for action – setting layouts size

Let's make our layout component use all the available space on the page:

1. Set the size of the `MainLayout` by adding the following line to the constructor:

    ```
    setSizeFull();
    ```

2. Set the size of the `lowerSection` and its components by adding the following to the `MainLayout` constructor:

    ```
    lowerSection.setSizeFull();
    menuLayout.setSizeFull();
    contentLayout.setSizeFull();
    ```

3. Run the application.

What just happened?

This is what happens to the layouts when we make them size full:

We are getting closer to our aim. However, there is still a gap between the header and the lower component.

Expand ratio

The lower section should expand to occupy the gap above it. How can we say "hey `lowerSection`, you must expand man"?

Time for action – expanding components

Follow these steps to get rid of that gap:

1. VerticalLayout (and other layouts too) has a method to specify how contained components should expand. Try adding this line to the MainLayout constructor:

   ```
   setExpandRatio(lowerSection, 1);
   ```

2. Run the application.

What just happened?

Take a look at the resulting layout:

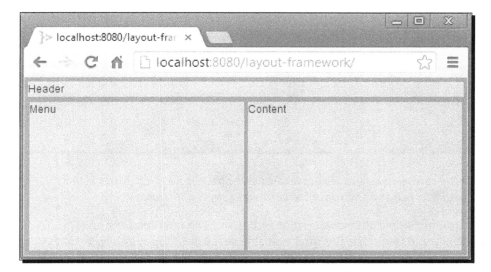

Think of expand ratios as the amount of space that some component can take inside its parent layout expressed as a ratio. Initially, upperSection and lowerSection had both an undefined expand ratio, which means that, to be fair, each could take at most 50 percent of the space in the parent layout. We haven't assigned any height for upperSection. Its height is undefined, so upperSection shrinks to use only the space it needs to hold the inner label showing the text **Header**. However, we assigned a height of 100 percent (by calling setSizeFull) to lowerSection, which means that it will occupy all the lower 50 percent of the space. Only the lower 50 percent, that's why we saw that gap between sections.

Now, after expanding `lowerSection`, it can occupy not 50 percent but more than that. How much? Suppose we expand `upperSection` to a ratio value of 2 while keeping `lowerSection` with an expand ratio of 1, like this:

```
setExpandRatio(upperSection, 2);
setExpandRatio(lowerSection, 1);
```

This is how the layout would look:

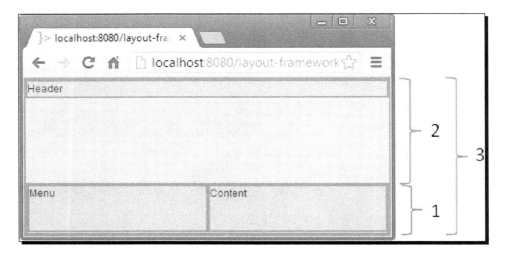

Oh, now we can see the light. The total available space is **2 + 1 = 3**. The space for `upperSection` is **2** and the space for `lowerSection` is **1**. That's it.

For the example application, we are not setting any expand ratio for `upperSection` tough. One could think that the total available space is **1**, `upperSection` takes **0**, and `lowerSection` takes **1**, ducking out the helpless `upperSection` component. Well, Vaadin is not that evil with our `upperSection` component and still lets it take the space it needs to happily exist.

Split panels

Split panels are interesting. They divide the layout in two parts and put a splitter in the middle. The splitter is like a draggable edge that allows users to adjust the size of the components.

Time for action – using split panels

Let's add a split panel to our application.

1. Change the `lowerSection`'s type to `HorizontalSplitPanel`:

```
public class MainLayout extends VerticalLayout {

    . . .

    private HorizontalSplitPanel lowerSection =
        new HorizontalSplitPanel();

    . . .
}
```

> Additional to `HorizontalSplitPanel` there is a `VerticalSplitPanel` class. We can infer the difference from the class name.

2. You could run the application right now and you will see a split panel instead of the previous horizontal layout. But let's make a little change before running the application. Add this line somewhere in the constructor of `MainLayout`:

```
lowerSection.setSplitPosition(30);
```

3. OK, you can run the application now.

What just happened?

Oh yeah, the application is looking good:

We have switched from `HorizontalLayout` to `HorizontalSplitPanel` and we've adjusted the splitter position using the `setSplitPosition` method with a value of 30 percent for the left component.

`setSplitPosition` is overloaded.

Method signature	Description
`setSplitPosition(float pos, boolean reverse)`	If reverse is true, the splitter position will be used for the second component not the first one.
`setSplitPosition(float pos, Unit unit)`	Unit is an enumeration giving alternative measurement units, such as points, picas, em, mm, cm, and so on.
`setSplitPosition(float pos, Unit unit, boolean reverse)`	A mix of the two previous cases.

Implementing a button-based menu

We are ready to implement the first public method of our framework. The method will allow clients to easily add options on the left menu and show the appropriate component when they are clicked.

Time for action – adding menu options

Follow these steps to add the buttons that will form the main menu of the application:

1. Add the following method to `MainLayout`:

```
public class MainLayout extends VerticalLayout {

  . . .

  public void addMenuOption(String caption,
      final Component component) {
    Button button = new Button(caption);
    menuLayout.addComponent(button);

    button.addClickListener(new ClickListener() {
      public void buttonClick(ClickEvent event) {
        contentLayout.removeAllComponents();
        contentLayout.addComponent(component);
      }
    });
  }
}
```

2. Comment out the line that set `menuLayout` to be full size:

```
public MainLayout() {

    . . .

    //menuLayout.setSizeFull(); you can delete this line ;)

    . . .

}
```

3. Change your `LayoutFrameworkUI` class to the following:

```
public class LayoutFrameworkUI extends UI {

    protected void init(VaadinRequest request) {
        MainLayout layout = new MainLayout();
        layout.addMenuOption("Option 1", new Label("Component 1"));
        layout.addMenuOption("Option 2", new Label("Component 2"));
        setContent(layout);
    }

}
```

4. Run the application and press the newborn buttons.

What just happened?

The `addMenuOption` method adds a button to `menuLayout`. This button has a listener that will replace the component in `contentLayout` accordingly:

Note that we are letting `menuLayout` have an undefined size, so the buttons will be displayed nicely. If we let `menuLayout` have 100 percent height, the application would look ugly when using bigger window sizes.

That happens because the buttons have an undefined size and we have not set any expand ratio for them, so they just distribute along the layout using a third of the available space (remember that we have one label and two buttons now, so each one can take one third of space).

Now that our framework is ready, let's use it to showcase some Vaadin layouts.

Have a go hero – add a public method to set the header

Try implementing a similar method to set the content of the `upperSection` layout.

Grid layouts

A grid layout arranges components in columns and rows. Let's see it in action.

Time for action – using grid layouts

Follow these steps to add a funny grid layout:

1. First, stop showing the blue borders for layouts by commenting out or deleting the following line (find it in `MainLayout`'s constructor):

    ```
    //showBorders();
    ```

2. Now, in the `LayoutFrameworkUI` class, add a `getGridLayout` method and call it from `init` to add the returned component to our `layout`:

    ```
    public class LayoutFrameworkUI extends UI {

        protected void init(VaadinRequest request) {

            ...

            layout.addMenuOption("Grid layout", getGridLayout());
        }

        private GridLayout getGridLayout() {
            int rows = 3, columns = 3;
            GridLayout gridLayout = new GridLayout(columns, rows);
            gridLayout.setSizeFull();

            for (int row = 0; row < rows; row++) {
                for (int column = 0; column < columns; column++) {
                    Button button = new Button("-_-");
                    gridLayout.addComponent(button, column, row);
                }
            }

            return gridLayout;
        }
    }
    ```

3. Run the application and click the **Grid layout** button to see the result.

What just happened?

Take a look at the grid layout we've just added:

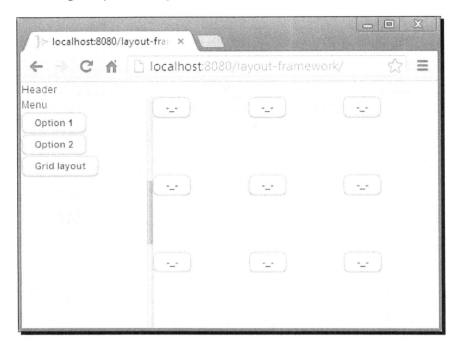

A `GridLayout` must have a size given in number of columns and rows. You can pass this size in the constructor call.

 You can also adjust the size after instantiation by using the methods `setColumns` and `setRows` of `GridLayout`. Moreover, you can grow or shrink the grid using these methods at any time.

To add components into a `GridLayout`, we have to specify where in the grid the component must be placed. We are doing so in the line:

```
gridLayout.addComponent(button, column, row);
```

This line adds a button using the current column and row of the `for` loop.

Have a go hero – open their eyes

Try implementing a listener on each button to show a different face when the button is clicked. For instance, the listener could change the caption of the button from -_- to °_°.

Have a go hero – expand components in GridLayout

Play with the methods `setRowExpandRatio` and `setColumnExpandRatio` of `GridLayout` to see how expand ratios work independently for each column and row.

Absolute layouts

Sometimes we need to place a component in a very specific and exact place of the page. That's the whole point of using `AbsoluteLayout`. For a `GridLayout` we have to give the position on the grid, for an `AbsoluteLayout` we have to give the position on the page. The position must be given using CSS format. For example, to place a component 20 pixels from left and 30 pixels form top, we can do this:

```
absoluteLayout.addComponent(someComponent, "left: 20px; top: 30px");
```

 You can use `top`, `left`, `right`, and `bottom` CSS identifiers to set the position of a component when using `AbsoluteLayout`. And of course, you can use any CSS unit such as `%`, `in`, `cm`, `mm`, `px`, `pt`, and so on.

Time for action – using absolute layouts

Let's use an absolute layout.

1. This is pretty straightforward. Change your `LayoutFrameworkUI` class to add the highlighted code:

```
public class LayoutFrameworkUI extends UI {

    protected void init(VaadinRequest request) {

        ...

        layout.addMenuOption("Absolut layout",
            getAbsolutLayout());
    }

    ...

    private Component getAbsolutLayout() {
        Button button = new Button(
            "I'm whimsically located at 42, 57");

        AbsoluteLayout absoluteLayout = new AbsoluteLayout();
```

```
        absoluteLayout.addComponent(button,
          "left: 42px; top: 57px");

        return absoluteLayout;
    }
}
```

2. Run and gun, oh, sorry, that's basketball. Run and test, that is software development, oh yeah.

What just happened?

As expected the button is located exactly at the pixel coordinates we dictated:

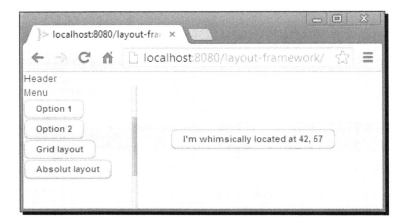

Click listeners

Layouts can listen to click events exactly the same as buttons. We can add a click listener to a layout so we can tell the user where the click happened.

Time for action – adding click listeners

Follow these steps to allow a `VerticalLayout` listen to click events:

1. Once again, add the highlighted code to your each time bigger (and it will grow more, you can tell) `LayoutFrameworkUI` class:

```
public class LayoutFrameworkUI extends UI {

    protected void init(VaadinRequest request) {

        . . .
```

```
        layout.addMenuOption("Click listener",
            getClickListener());
    }

    ...

    private Component getClickListener() {
        VerticalLayout layout = new VerticalLayout();
        layout.setSizeFull();
        layout.addLayoutClickListener(new LayoutClickListener() {
            public void layoutClick(LayoutClickEvent event) {
                String message = "And you did it at "
                    + event.getClientX() + ", "
                    + event.getClientY();
                Notification.show("You clicked me!", message,
                    Type.TRAY_NOTIFICATION);
            }
        });

        return layout;
    }
}
```

2. Run the application, click on **Click listener**, and perform some clicks over the invisible VerticalLayout.

What just happened?

Simple, we've added a LayoutClickListener to our layout. The event passed to the listener has some information about the performed click. We are showing the location of the mouse relative to the browser:

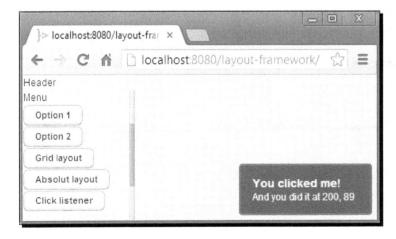

By the way, did you notice the notification style? Type is a Java enumeration that allows you to display different kinds of notifications. Besides that, we are using a caption (**You clicked me!**) and a description (**And you did it at...**) for the notification.

Have a go hero – get more data from click events

Try showing more information from the `LayoutClickEvent` class. For example, you can get the name of the mouse button used for clicking by calling `event.getButtonName()`.

Form layouts

Up to now, our input components such as text fields and combo boxes, have had captions rendered on top of the component:

`FormLayout` changes that by rendering captions to the left of the component:

Time for action – using FormLayout

Using `FormLayout` is quite simple, it works similar to `VerticalLayout`.

1. Modify your LayoutFrameworkUI class to match the highlighted code:

```
public class LayoutFrameworkUI extends UI {

    protected void init(VaadinRequest request) {

        . . .

        layout.addMenuOption("Form layout", getFormLayout());
    }

    . . .

    private FormLayout getFormLayout() {
```

```
TextField tf1 = new TextField("TextField");
TextField tf2 = new TextField("TextField");
ComboBox cb = new ComboBox("ComboBox");
Button b = new Button("Button");

FormLayout formLayout = new FormLayout(tf1, tf2, cb, b);
formLayout.setMargin(true);

return formLayout;
    }

  }
```

2.   Run the application.

What just happened?

This is how our fields look inside a FormLayout:

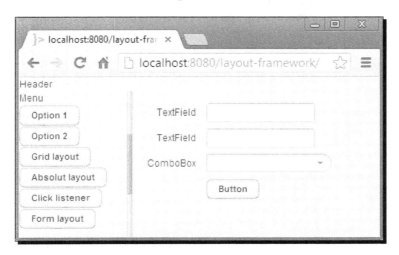

As you can see all the fields, except for **Button**, have their captions to the left. It looks like two columns, one for the captions, and one for the fields. This kind of layout is almost always the best way to show forms.

Something to note in this last example, is how we used the constructor of FormLayout to immediately add the components to the layout:

```
FormLayout formLayout = new FormLayout(tf1, tf2, cb, b);
```

This line of code not only instantiates a new FormLayout, but also adds the tf1, tf2, cb, and b components.

 FormLayout is not the only layout having a constructor with varargs to pass contained components. Some other Vaadin layouts have similar constructors. For instance, VerticalLayout and HorizontalLayout have a constructor like this.

Panels

A Panel is a container for a single component useful to display scrollable content. You can programmatically control the scrolling and you can optionally add a caption and a title for the panel.

Time for action – using panels

Let's add a panel using our framework application.

1. In LayoutFrameworkUI class, add a getPanel method and call it from the init method to add the returned component to our main layout:

```
public class LayoutFrameworkUI extends UI {

  protected void init(VaadinRequest request) {

    . . .

    layout.addMenuOption("Panel", getPanel());
  }

  . . .

  private Panel getPanel() {
    String someNumbers = "";

    for (int i = 0; i < 2000; i++) {
      someNumbers += " " + i;
    }

    Label content = new Label(someNumbers);
    Panel panel = new Panel("Panel's caption", content);
```

```
        panel.setWidth("200px");
        panel.setHeight("100px");
        panel.setScrollTop(3000); // pixels from top

        return panel;
    }

  }
```

2. Run it!

What just happened?

Here is a screenshot of the application showing the panel:

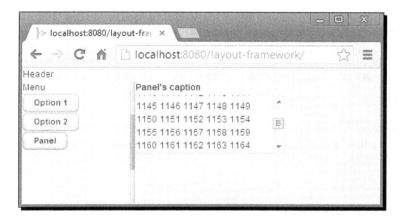

Let's take a closer look at how we created the `panel` instance. First, we created a `String` with a lot of numbers in it. Then, we created a new `Label` as usual using the numbers as text. Finally, we created the `Panel`:

```
Panel panel = new Panel("Panel's caption", content);
```

We are passing the panel's caption and the component that it will hold, that is, the label.

> You can set the content of a `Panel` after instantiation by using the `setContent` method. For example, we could have added the label by calling `panel.setContent(content);`.

Once we have the `panel` instance ready, we set the size as we've already learned some pages ago. To demonstrate that we can control the scroll from our code, we called:

```
panel.setScrollTop(3000);
```

This scrolls down the panel by 3000 pixels.

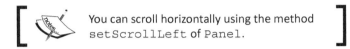 You can scroll horizontally using the method `setScrollLeft` of `Panel`.

Tab sheets

A `TabSheet` allows users to alternate between views by using tabs. A user only sees the content of one tab at a time. Tabbed views are useful to logically break content up so users can more comfortably work with some components in a large area than if we put all the components in a single view.

To create an empty tab sheet, instantiate a new `TabSheet` object like this:

```
TabSheet tabs = new TabSheet();
```

You have two ways to add tabs. You can use the `addTab` method that takes two parameters, the first is the component that will go inside the tab, and the second is the title for the tab itself:

```
tabs.addTab(new Label("Label 1"), "Tabl 1");
```

Or you can use the `addTab` method that takes only one parameter, the component to add inside the tab. This method returns a `Tab` object representing the added tab. `Tab`, in turn, has a method to set the caption for the tab it represents:

```
tabs.addTab(new Label("Label 2")).setCaption("Tab 2");
```

This last one is similar to this:

```
Tab tab = tabs.addTab(new Label("Label 3"));
tab.setCaption("Tab 3");
```

All these tabs are rendered like this:

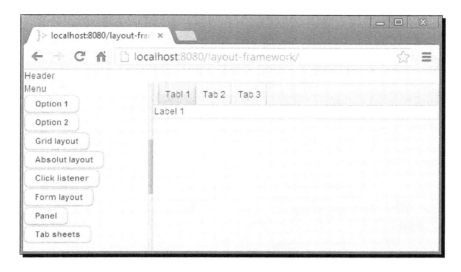

You can let users close your tabs:

```
tab.setClosable(true);
```

A close button will be rendered next to the tab's caption:

TabSheet can listen to SelectedTabChangeEvent. It's nice when you can infer the purpose of something only by reading the name of a class. You inferred it, right? Of course, the selected tab is changing and we can add our own logic every time it happens:

```
tabs.addSelectedTabChangeListener(new SelectedTabChangeListener() {
    public void selectedTabChange(
        SelectedTabChangeEvent event) {
      Notification.show("You are watching "
        + event.getTabSheet().getSelectedTab());
    }
});
```

This will show a notification each time the user changes the active tab.

Accordions

If you know `TabSheet`, you already know `Accordion`. Really, they work exactly the same. To demonstrate this fact, let's take the code in the previous `TabSheet` example and change the corresponding identifiers to use `Accordion` instead of `TabSheet`.

```
Accordion accordion = new Accordion();
accordion.addTab(new Label("Label 1"), "Tabl 1");
accordion.addTab(new Label("Label 2")).setCaption("Tab 2");
Tab tab = accordion.addTab(new Label("Label 3"));
tab.setCaption("Tab 3");
tab.setClosable(true);

accordion
    .addSelectedTabChangeListener(new SelectedTabChangeListener() {
        public void selectedTabChange(
            SelectedTabChangeEvent event) {
          Notification.show("You are watching "
              + event.getTabSheet().getSelectedTab());
        }
    });
```

Everything works as expected. You can add tabs using the same techniques described before and you can register the same `SelectedTabChangeListener`. Here is a screenshot of the just developed accordion:

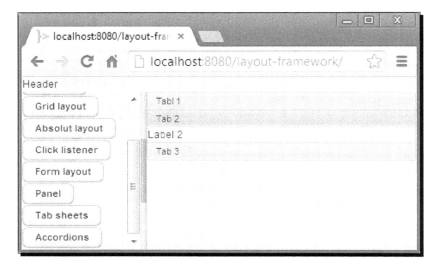

Have a go hero – find the disobedient line of code

Gotcha! In the previous code, there is one line of code that doesn't work for `Accordion` and indeed it worked for the `TabSheet`. Can you tell what line is it? If you can't find it, try writing the code by yourself. You'll eventually get to the disobedient line of code. If you found it before me, what an outstanding reader!

Windows

A Window is a visual area that floats over the page. You can easily add windows to your `UI` class:

```
Window w1 = new Window("Default window");
addWindow(w1); // from UI class
```

Once the window is added, it will majestically appear on the screen:

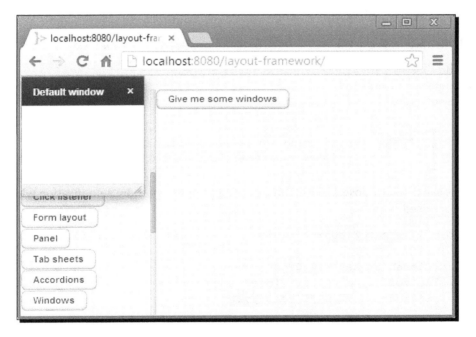

You can disable the close button of the window:

```
Window w2 = new Window("You can't close this window, sorry");
w2.setClosable(false);
```

Or you can fix the size of the window and ban future size changes:

```
Window w3 = new Window("You can't resize me, ha-ha");
w3.setWidth("200px");
w3.setHeight("100px");
w3.setResizable(false);
```

As you can see, sizing is done as usual with the setWidth and setHeight methods.

Usually the content of a window is some kind of layout; however, you can set any component as the window content. Here, we are using a label:

```
Window w4 = new Window("I have a Label inside");
w4.setContent(new Label("I'm that Label."));
```

You can also disable window dragging:

```
Window w5 = new Window(
    "You can't drag me :( but you can close me :)");
w5.setDraggable(false);
```

To position a window use the setPositionX and setPositionY methods:

```
Window w6 = new Window("I'm at 300, 5");
w6.setPositionX(300);
w6.setPositionY(5);
```

 You can use the center method to automatically move the window to the center of the parent component.

Windows can listen to close events. The following snippet will show a notification when the window is closed:

```
Window w7 = new Window("Beware... I can hear when you close me");

w7.addCloseListener(new CloseListener() {
  public void windowClose(CloseEvent e) {
    Notification.show("I hear you!");
  }
});
```

You can add modal windows, so the user won't be able to use the components behind the window:

```
Window w8 = new Window("I'm modal, close me to continue");
w8.setModal(true);
```

Take a look at a screenshot of a modal window:

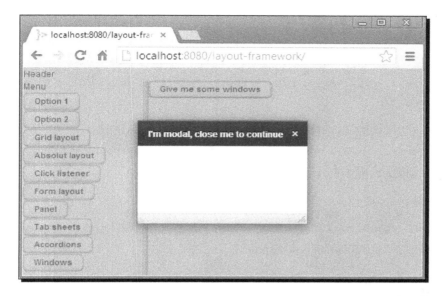

Pop quiz – mastering layouts

One more Vaadin weapon is in your belt now. Let's check your knowledge level:

Q1. Which of the following is not a Vaadin layout?

1. VerticalLayout.
2. HorizontalLayout.
3. AbsoluteLayout.
4. GridLayout.
5. FormLayout.
6. FreeLayout.

Q2. Which of the following is not a component to arrange other components?

1. Accordion.
2. TabSheet.
3. Tab.
4. VerticalSplitPanel.
5. HorizontalSplitPanel.

Q3. When you use `component.setWidth("100%")`, component will:

1. Take all the horizontal space in the page.

2. Take all the horizontal space in the parent component.

Q4. Suppose you have two components, `c1`, and `c2`, inside a `VerticalLayout`, `vl`. If you call `vl.setExpandRatio(c1, 1)` and `vl.setExpandRatio(c2, 2)`, which one is correct:

1. `c1` will occupy 10 percent of space and `c2` will take 20 percent.

2. `c1` will occupy 100 percent of space and `c2` will take 200 percent.

3. `c1` will occupy 1/3 of space and `c2` will take 2/3.

Q5. Only `AbsoluteLayout` can listen to `LayoutClickEvent`. That is:

1. True, because you can place components in any point using `AbsolutLayout`.

2. False, because Vaadin is awesome.

Summary

We covered some really useful components in this chapter. This is what we have covered:

- We learned how layout components are used to arrange other components, even layout themselves.

- We learned how to use `HorizontalLayout`, `AbsoluteLayout`, `GridLayout`, and `FormLayout`.

- We added listeners to handle click events on layouts.

- We learned how `HorizontalSplitPanel`, `VerticalSplitPanel`, `Panel`, `TabSheet`, and `Accordion`, let us arrange components in very flexible ways.

- We learned many features of Window, such as limiting resizing and dragging, setting the position programmatically, listening to close events, and using modal windows.

This chapter showed you many features of Vaadin layouts. Now you can arrange your components as you wish. Next chapter, we will discover Vaadin navigation capabilities, so stay there!

4
Using Vaadin Navigation Capabilities

Historically, **Rich Internet Applications (RIA)** *was suitable mostly for corporate applications deployed and used inside companies' intranets. Trend is changing and Vaadin is aware of that. No more "we can't use Vaadin because we are developing a website-like application". With Vaadin, developing website-like applications is a piece of cake. You can make rich web applications and still let your visitors use navigator's back and forward buttons and allow search engines to find and index your Vaadin applications.*

In this chapter we will cover the following topics:

- ◆ Getting request information
- ◆ URL Path info, fragments and parameters
- ◆ VaadinService class
- ◆ Navigators and views
- ◆ Keeping state after refresh
- ◆ User session
- ◆ Menus
- ◆ Shortcut keys

We are ready to acquire some powerful skills to succeed as Vaadin web application developers. You don't want to miss this chapter!

Getting request information

When we talk about a request to a web application, we are talking about an HTTP request that a browser makes to our server. The server will take the context path and route the request to the appropriate application. An important part of the HTTP request is the URL used to access the application and its resources. To better digest the knowledge contained in this chapter, let's see some important parts of a URL:

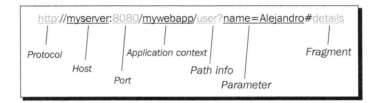

We will learn how to take advantage of the three last ones (path info, parameter, and fragment) in order to develop navigable applications with Vaadin.

Path info

If we can use Vaadin to develop website-like applications, we must be able to build a simple website like the following:

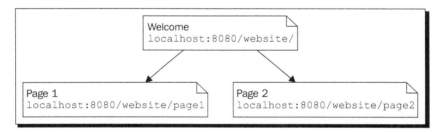

This is a website consisting of three pages:

◆ **Welcome**: The default Vaadin component shown when the last part of the URL is empty. This is what we have done in the previous chapters.

◆ **Page 1**: A Vaadin component shown when the URL finishes with `page1`.

◆ **Page 2**: A Vaadin component shown when the URL finishes with `page2`.

Time for action – developing a simple website

Let's see how we can do this using Vaadin.

1. Start up your IDE and create a new Vaadin project. We are using **website** as project name.

2. Code your UI class as shown in the following code snippet:

```java
public class WebsiteUI extends UI {

    protected void init(VaadinRequest request) {
        final VerticalLayout layout = new VerticalLayout();
        layout.setMargin(true);
        setContent(layout);

        String page = request.getPathInfo();

        if (page == null || page.isEmpty() || "/".equals(page)) {
            layout.addComponent(new Label("Welcome to Simple Web
                Site"));
            getPage().setTitle("Simple Web Site");

        } else if ("/page1".equals(page)) {
            layout.addComponent(
                new Label("Oh yeah! You are watching Page 1!"));
            getPage().setTitle("Simple Web Site - Page 1");

        } else if ("/page2".equals(page)) {
            layout.addComponent(new Label("Yay! This is Page 2!"));
            getPage().setTitle("Simple Web Site - Page 2");

        } else {
            layout.addComponent(new Label(
                "You just got 404'd! The requested page doesn't
                    exist."));
            getPage().setTitle("Simple Web Site - 404!");
        }
    }
}
```

3. Run your application and browse to `http://localhost:8080/website/`, `http://localhost:8080/website/page1`, `http://localhost:8080/website/page2`, and `http://localhost:8080/website/page100`. Yeah, the last one will show the funny 404 message.

404 is an HTTP error code meaning that the server could not find the requested resource. In the previous example we are not returning a 404 error for real, we are just showing a funny message. Usually, web servers have a customizable web page to be shown when a 404 error is detected.

What just happened?

We are adding a different component accordingly to the URL ending. For example, if we navigate to `http://localhost:8080/website/page2`, the application will show the following:

We are getting the `/page2` part of the URL on the browser by calling this:

```
String page = request.getPathInfo();
```

 You can get a `VaadinRequest` reference from any part of your code (including non Vaadin classes) by using the `VaadinService` class:

```
VaadinRequest request = VaadinService.
getCurrentRequest();
```

A `request` variable of type `VaadinRequest` is always passed to the `init` method of your `UI` class. VaadinRequest encapsulates a request from the browser to the server. In the previous example, we were using the `getPathInfo` method to query the last part of the entered URL.

What happens if we navigate to `http://localhost:8080/website/page2/section1`? This happens:

That means that `getPathInfo` is returning `page2/section1` which is not recognized by our `if` statements. We are not doing so, but if we needed to, we could process the returned path info string to show the appropriate components when necessary.

Using this technique we can dynamically show content according to the specified URL with total flexibility.

I remember developing a web application with tons of different pages, each one offering a single service to the end user. We needed to provide a dynamic authorization mechanism, that is, an administrator user could grant or revoke access to services at runtime for different users.

We solved that by coding a cool authorization system where we had users, groups, and services stored separately in a database, each one in its own table. We let a user have many groups and a group have many services. A service contained a URL to access the service, so we could easily check whether some user could access a given URL or not. We could even be able to render a nice menu at runtime using the information stored in the tables.

Parameters

What if we want to build the user interface according to a parameter in the URL? Instead of accessing Page 2 by appending `page2` to the URL, we want to access it by adding `?page=2`. You can think of this as passing parameters to the web application. The parameter's name is `page` with a value of `2` in the previous example. Not a big deal. Let's do it.

Time for action – reading request parameters

Follow these steps and see how easy it is to use request parameters in Vaadin:

1. Create a new Vaadin project. We are using **website2** as project name.

2. Code your UI class shown as follows:

```
public class Website2UI extends UI {

  protected void init(VaadinRequest request) {
    final VerticalLayout layout = new VerticalLayout();
    layout.setMargin(true);
    setContent(layout);

    String page = request.getParameter("page");

    if (page == null) {
      layout.addComponent(new Label("Welcome to Simple Web
        Site"));
      getPage().setTitle("Simple Web Site");

    } else if ("1".equals(page)) {
      layout.addComponent(
          new Label("Oh yeah! You are watching Page 1!"));
      getPage().setTitle("Simple Web Site - Page 1");

    } else if ("2".equals(page)) {
      layout.addComponent(new Label("Yay! This is Page 2!"));
      getPage().setTitle("Simple Web Site - Page 2");

    } else {
      getPage().setTitle("Simple Web Site - 404!");
      layout.addComponent(new Label(
          "You just got 404'd! The requested page doesn't
            exist."));
    }
  }
}
```

3. Run your application and browse to `http://localhost:8080/website/`, `http://localhost:8080/website2/?page=1`, `http://localhost:8080/website2/?page=2`, and `http://localhost:8080/website2/?page=100`.

What just happened?

Now we are adding the components according to a parameter in the URL. For example, if we navigate to `http://localhost:8080/website2?page=1`, the application will show the following:

The question mark is used to separate the parameters from the rest of the URL elements. If you need to pass more than one parameter, you must separate them using the ampersand symbol. For example, if you want to pass `page`, `name`, and `id` parameters, you can do it like this:

`http://localhost:8080/mywebapp/?page=1&name=Alejandro&id=20`

Fragments

In short, the fragment is that part of the URL that comes after #. For example, we could modify our previous application to show Page 1 or Page 2 according to the fragment specified, so the user can access Page 1 at `http://localhost:8080/website2/#1`, and Page 2 at `http://localhost:8080/website2/#1`. All we need to do is get the fragment and we can get the fragment extremely easily:

```
String fragment = getPage().getUriFragment();
```

Wait! Yeah, the fragment part is pretty easy but what is that `getPage` method hanging around in the examples? Are you pulling my leg or something?

Not at all! Let's see that missing part right away. Every `UI` instance is associated to a `Page` instance. A `Page` encapsulates the browser and the page it shows. For example, one particularly useful method in `Page` is `getWebBrowser`:

```
WebBrowser browser = getPage().getWebBrowser();
```

`WebBrowser` has methods to get all you ever wanted to know about the browser running your application.

Have a go hero – take a look at the Vaadin API documentation

It's never a waste to take a look at the API of the frameworks you are using. They are full of knowledge and could teach you valuable secrets. Go to the Vaadin API website and grasp some knowledge by learning some of the powerful methods of the `WebBrowser` class. Specially, look for the `getAddress`, `getScreenWidth`, `getScreenHeight`, and `isTouchDevice` methods. Here is the portal to the knowledge: `https://vaadin.com/api/`.

Changing the browser title

Did you notice that the browser windows now have a convenient title? At last! Almost half the book and we haven't changed the title for any application! Here is how you change the text shown in the browser's title:

```
getPage().setTitle("My title");
```

You can get a fresh and hot reference to your `UI` class with the static method `UI.getCurrent` from any part of your code. For example you can change the page title using this:

```
UI.getCurrent().getPage().setTitle("Title");
```

Moreover, you can do it more easily by calling:

```
Page.getCurrent().setTitle("Title");
```

Navigators and views

Navigators are architectural sugar. In previous examples we have coded all the navigable components in line. For instance, Page 1 and Page 2 are merely labels. In real Vaadin applications for men and women, we would need to code a complete class for a page, maybe several classes. So Page 1 would need its own class. The same happens for **Welcome** page and Page 2. The web developer will start scratching her or his head more frequently as more classes (pages) are added to the application. Complexity will grow to the point that maintaining the application would let our developers bald. Vaadin worries about programmers' hair (or skin if they are bald) and have incorporated the `Navigator` class and `View` interface.

Time for action – using navigators

Let's pour some architectural sugar:

1. Create a new Vaadin project. We are using *navigator* as project name.

2. Implement a `view` for the **Welcome** page:

```
public class Welcome extends VerticalLayout implements View {
  public Welcome() {
    addComponent(new Label("Welcome"));
  }

  @Override
  public void enter(ViewChangeEvent event) {
    Notification.show("Showing Welcome page");
  }

}
```

3. Implement a view for the `Page1` class:

```
public class Page1 extends VerticalLayout implements View {

  public Page1() {
    addComponent(new Label("Page 1"));
  }

  @Override
  public void enter(ViewChangeEvent event) {
    Notification.show("Showing page 1");
  }

}
```

4. Use the previous `Page1` class to implement a `Page2` class. Don't forget to change the label content and the notification accordingly.

5. Now, change your `UI` class to this:

```
public class NavigatorUI extends UI {

  protected void init(VaadinRequest request) {
    Navigator navigator = new Navigator(this, this);

    navigator.addView("", new Welcome());
    navigator.addView("page1", new Page1());
    navigator.addView("page2", new Page2());
  }
}
```

6. Compile, run and browse to `http://localhost:8080/navigator/`, `http://localhost:8080/navigator/#!page1`, and `http://localhost:8080/navigator/#!page2`. (Note the `#!` part).

What just happened?

First, we implemented one component for each page we needed to show. In this example each page is a `VerticalLayout`, but we could have extended any Vaadin `UI` component. Each component implementing the `View` interface can be added to a `Navigator`. This forces us to implement the `enter` method of `View`. This method will be called when the view is shown.

Once we have our pages, we created a `Navigator` in our `UI` class and added all the three views:

```
navigator.addView("", new Welcome());
navigator.addView("page1", new Page1());
navigator.addView("page2", new Page2());
```

The first parameter of `addView` is the fragment to use and the second is the component to show (that must implement `View`, of course). The `Navigator` class will manage the fragments and show the corresponding component when needed. For example, if we navigate to: `http://localhost:8080/navigator/#!page1`, we will see this:

Notice that we need to add an exclamation mark after the hash mark (**#!**). This makes the page to be considered **AJAX crawlable** by search engines. In Vaadin you will need to provide some extra information to make your page crawlable. This topic is outside of the book's scope. Please refer to the official Vaadin documentation to get hints on doing your pages fully crawlable.

For more information on web crawling support in Vaadin applications take a look at `https://vaadin.com/book/vaadin7/-/page/advanced.urifu.html#advanced.urifu.crawling`.

Time for action – navigating programmatically

1. Our website is ready to include some links on it. We will add links to Page 1 and Page 2 inside the **Welcome** page.

2. We want to add links to the **Welcome** page, so we need to edit `Welcome.java`. First we need a `navigator` to navigate to the other pages (we will initialize this `navigator` instance later):

```
public class Welcome extends VerticalLayout implements View {

    private Navigator navigator;

    // ...

}
```

3. We are adding buttons and a button without a click listener is like a heart without a beat (seems to be that writer is getting crazy again). So let's code a `listener` that calls our `navigator`:

```
public class Welcome extends VerticalLayout implements View {

    // ...

    public Welcome() {
        ClickListener listener = new ClickListener() {
            @Override
            public void buttonClick(ClickEvent event) {
                navigator.navigateTo(event.getButton().getCaption());
            }
        };

        // ...

    }
}
```

4. Now we have our click listener and a click listener without a button is like a plane that doesn't fly. So let's create the buttons:

```
public class Welcome extends VerticalLayout implements View {

    // ...

    public Welcome() {

        // ...
        Button goToPage1 = new Button("page1");
        Button goToPage2 = new Button("page2");

        goToPage1.addClickListener(listener);
```

```
        goToPage2.addClickListener(listener);

        goToPage1.setStyleName(BaseTheme.BUTTON_LINK);
        goToPage2.setStyleName(BaseTheme.BUTTON_LINK);
        addComponent(new Label("Welcome"));
        addComponent(goToPage1);
        addComponent(goToPage2);
    }

    // ...

}
```

5. Finally, we don't like NullPointerException, do we? Let's initialize our navigator instance then:

```
public class Welcome extends VerticalLayout implements View {

    // ...

    @Override
    public void enter(ViewChangeEvent event) {

        // ...

        navigator = event.getNavigator();
    }

}
```

6. Play with it.

What just happened?

Here you have a screenshot of the **Welcome** page:

First, note that the buttons are not rendered as buttons. We added a CSS style to change their appearance:

```
goToPage1.setStyleName(BaseTheme.BUTTON_LINK);
goToPage2.setStyleName(BaseTheme.BUTTON_LINK);
```

Second, when you click the links, you get the respective page. Our click listener just takes the caption of the button (**page1** or **page2**) and uses it to navigate to the appropriate page by calling the `navigateTo` method. For example, to navigate to Page 1, we can do:

```
navigator.navigateTo("page1");
```

You can see how the fragment part of the URL changes in your browser when you click the links. And you know what? You can use the browser's back and forward buttons. We are supporting them now! That's good.

Keeping state after refresh

By default, every time you reload the application on the browser, the `init` method will be called and all the components will be created again. That means that on every refresh, the components will lose their stored values, or more generally, your application won't preserve its state. For example, if we have an application with a `TextField` and the user types some text on it before using the infamous refresh button in the browser, the text previously typed in the `TextField` will be lost forever. The same happens with navigators, as each time we navigate to a view, a refresh will happen in the browser.

In order to preserve the state in our Vaadin applications, we have to create a database and store the value for every component we create and every user we have... Just kidding! Preserving the state in Vaadin applications is one of the easiest tasks to do in the history of mankind. Let's see it in action.

Time for action – preserving application state

Follow these steps to see how easy it is to preserve the state of UI components in Vaadin applications:

1. Create a new Vaadin project. We are using **keepstate** as project name.

2. Code your `UI` class:

```
public class KeepstateUI extends UI {

    protected void init(VaadinRequest request) {
        final VerticalLayout layout = new VerticalLayout();
        layout.setMargin(true);
        setContent(layout);
```

```
TextField tf = new TextField(
    "Type, press ENTER, and refresh the browser");
tf.setImmediate(true);

tf.addValueChangeListener(new ValueChangeListener() {
  public void valueChange(ValueChangeEvent event) {
    Notification.show(
        "Value: " + event.getProperty().getValue());
  }
});

layout.addComponent(tf);
  }

}
```

3. Nothing new so far. Run the application, type some text in the text field, and press *Enter*. You will see something like this:

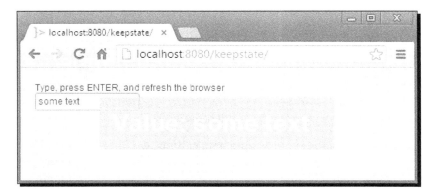

4. Now, refresh the browser and watch out how **some text** is gone:

5. What we want is to keep **some text** in their place, where it was born and where it belongs. So let's add the magic. One simple non-executable elegant auto-explanatory line of code:

```
@PreserveOnRefresh
public class KeepstateUI extends UI {

    // ...

}
```

6. Run the application again, type `some text`, press *Enter*, and refresh the browser. Now **some text** is still there:

What just happened?

By marking a `UI` class with `@PreserveOnRefresh`, Vaadin will not call the `init` method but will store a copy of the previously instantiated `UI` object.

Suppose you are developing a Vaadin application that preserves its state. You have a lot of components that appear and disappear at runtime. Suddenly, you realize that you need to test your application from start, without any state at all, like if the user just started to use the application. You can't delete the state by refreshing now. How can you reset the application? Here is how:

```
http://localhost:8080/keepstate/?restartApplication
```

All you need to do is to append `?restartApplication` at the end of the URL in your browser.

Where does Vaadin store that `UI` instance? In the **user session**. In the what?

User session

A **user session** is like a place that Java web applications use to store data about each user. Each time a user access the application, a new session object is assigned to it. That means that each user has its own session. A session allows us to identify a user. It is a temporal storage where we (and Vaadin) can put data relevant to a user.

 Because sessions are temporal, we can configure their lifetime (or timeout) in web.xml:

```
<web-app ...>
  ...
  <session-config>
    <session-timeout>20</session-timeout>
  </session-config>
</web-app>
```

 Here, each session will last 20 minutes since the last time the user requested something to the server.

Vaadin automatically preserves the state of UI components (if @preserveOnRefresh is present) by storing the required UI data into the user session. We don't have to worry about preserving UI components state. However we can still use the user session to store stuff not covered by any UI component. For example, we could store the user's name in the session to use it later in some other parts of the application.

The most common way to store some object in the session is by using the setAttribute of VaadinSession. For example, we can save the string a user typed in a TextField (tf) using this:

```
VaadinSession.getCurrent().setAttribute("the name", tf.getValue());
```

Later, we can get the stored value using this line of code:

```
String name = (String) VaadinSession.getCurrent()
    .getAttribute("the name");
```

Menus

It's time for more concrete less abstract stuff. Let's talk about menus. Menus are a way to group functionality in a very small area of the page. The first step to create a menu, is to instantiate a new MenuBar:

```
MenuBar menuBar = new MenuBar();
```

Now, we can add a hierarchy of instances of `MenuItem`. To add items directly to the menu bar, you can do this:

```
MenuItem submenu1 = menuBar.addItem("Submenu 1", null);
MenuItem submenu2 = menuBar.addItem("Submenu 2", null);
```

This will show the following menu:

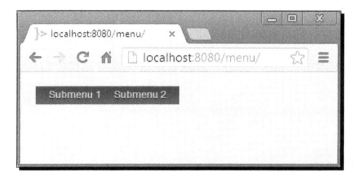

We can add child elements to the submenus:

```
submenu1.addItem("Option 1", null);
submenu1.addItem("Option 2", null);

submenu2.addItem("Option 3", null);
submenu2.addItem("Option 4", null);
```

Now our submenus have options:

You can continue and add child items to the options, and child items to the child items, and so forth.

Adding behavior when an item is selected is kind of similar to adding a click listener to a button. We need to add a `Command` instance (instead of a `ClickListener`) and we can do it directly in the `addItem` method:

```
submenu2.addItem("Option 4", new Command() {
  @Override
  public void menuSelected(MenuItem selectedItem) {
    Notification.show("That was option 4");
  }
});
```

That will show a notification when the option 4 is clicked.

Shortcut keys

Shortcut keys highly improve user experience by making the application more fluid and user friendly.

Shortcuts for buttons

Imagine a user having to fill a form several times, one after another. Let's create an application that simulates that scenario.

Time for action – a tedious application

Follow these steps to create a tedious to use application:

1. Create a new Vaadin project. We are using **shortcut** as project name.

2. Code your `UI` class:

```
public class ShortcutUI extends UI {

  protected void init(VaadinRequest request) {
    final VerticalLayout layout = new VerticalLayout();
    layout.setMargin(true);
    layout.setSpacing(true);
    setContent(layout);

    final TextField tf = new TextField("Your data:");
```

```
     layout.addComponent(tf);

     Button button = new Button("Send data (ENTER)");

     button.addClickListener(new Button.ClickListener() {
       public void buttonClick(ClickEvent event) {
         layout.addComponent(new Label(tf.getValue()));
         tf.setValue("");
       }
     });

     layout.addComponent(button);
   }

}
```

3. Run the application and try to send many data.

What just happened?

If you continue using the application for a long time, one of two things will happen: Your hand will start to feel tired because of the huge amount of clicks you have to do, or your *Tab* key will have lost its label on the keyboard.

Have a go hero – improve user experience

There are two things we can do to save our hands and our *Tab* keys. First, we can automatically set the focus for the text field once data is sent. Try it! Add the highlighted code to your UI class:

```
public class ShortcutUI extends UI {

  protected void init(VaadinRequest request) {

    // ...

    button.addClickListener(new Button.ClickListener() {
      public void buttonClick(ClickEvent event) {

        // ...
        tf.focus();
      }
```

```
        });

        // ...

    }

}
```

The other thing we can do, is to add the promised *Enter* shortcut key for the button. Try it! Add the highlighted code to your UI class and enjoy sending tons of data:

```
public class ShortcutUI extends UI {

    protected void init(VaadinRequest request) {

        // ...

        Button button = new Button("Send data (ENTER)");
        button.setClickShortcut(KeyCode.ENTER);

        // ...

    }

}
```

> You can easily add modifiers such as *Shift*, *Alt*, or *Ctrl*:
>
> ```
> button.setClickShortcut(KeyCode.ENTER,
> ModifierKey.SHIFT);
> ```

Shortcuts for Window and Panel

You can add generic shortcuts for `Window` and `Panel` objects. To do that, you must implement a `Handler`. You must implement two methods: `getActions`, and `handleAction`. The `getActions` method must return an array of `Actions`. `handleAction` will be called when the user performs an action. Here is an example implementation of a `Handler`:

```
Handler handler = new Handler() {

    @Override
    public Action[] getActions(Object target, Object sender) {
```

```
    return new Action[] {
        new ShortcutAction("Enter", KeyCode.ENTER, null),
        new ShortcutAction("Shift + U", KeyCode.U,
            new int[] { ModifierKey.SHIFT }) };
}

@Override
public void handleAction(Action action, Object sender, Object
    target) {
  Notification.show(action.getCaption());
}

};
```

 ShortcutAction is an implementation of Action to handle keyboard actions.

You can add a Handler only to Window and Panel. For example, let say we have a panel instance and we want to add the previous handler:

```
panel.addActionHandler(handler);
```

Now, the application will show a message when an action is performed by the user:

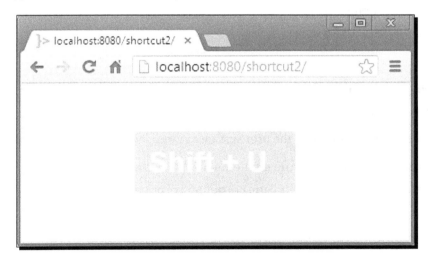

Pop quiz – navigation capabilities

It's time to check your knowledge:

Q1. Which class would you use to get the path information?

1. `VaadinService`.
2. `VaadinPath`.
3. `VaadinRequest`.

Q2. Which class and method would you use to get a parameter value passed in the URL?

1. `VaadinService` and `getParameter`.
2. `VaadinService` and `getPage`.
3. `VaadinRequest` and `getParameter`.
4. `VaadinRequest` and `getPage`.

Q3. If you need an instance of `Page` outside your `UI` implementation, which sounds good to you (hint: two of them are right)?

1. `UI.getCurrent().getPage()`.
2. `UI.getPage()`.
3. `Page.getCurrent()`.
4. `UI.getCurrentPage()`.

Q4. Which one is true about navigators?

1. You can add instances of `Component` to `Navigator`.
2. You can add instances of `View` to `Navigator`.

Q5. If you need a value stored in the user session as `name`, how would you manage to get it?

1. `VaadinService.getCurrentRequest().getParameter("name")`.
2. `VaadinSession.getCurrent().getAttribute("name")`.

Summary

This was a short but juicy chapter. Take a look at what we have learned:

- We learned how to get path info, parameters, and fragments in the URL by using the `VaadinRequest.getPathInfo`, `VaadinRequest.getParamenter`, and `Page.getUriFragment` methods.

- We learned how to get a referent to the current `VaadinRequest` by calling `VaadinService.getCurrentRequest()`.

- We learned how navigators make it easy to implement navigation capabilities through fragments by adding instances of `View` to a `Navigator`.

- We learned how easy it is to preserve state in Vaadin applications by using the `@PreserveOnRefresh` annotation in our `UI` implementations.

- We learned how to identify users and store related data by using `VaadinSession`.

- We learned how to use menus and key shortcuts.

Congratulations. Knowledge acquired. You are ready for the next chapter where we will be covering a really interesting topic: *Tables and trees*. See ya!

5
Using Tables – Time to Talk to Users

*Tables are one of the most common ways of presenting large datasets. Vaadin comes with a **Table** component worth learning about.*

In this chapter we will cover the following topics:

◆ Tables

◆ Headers

◆ Footers

◆ Page length

◆ Selecting items in tables

◆ Reading data from tables

◆ Editable tables

◆ Table field factories

◆ Generated columns

◆ Collapsing and reordering columns

It's time to learn one of the awesome components of Vaadin. You have to definitely master in tables, and this chapter is just about that. Get ready to get full knowledge of this versatile and useful UI component!

Tables

So you have tons-and-tons of data willing to be shown in a table? Maybe an SQL query result or a list of items gathered from a web service. Maybe just a couple of rows with some relevant information. Let's see how hard (actually, how easy) it is to show a simple table with Vaadin.

Time for action – my first table

Following are the steps to create your first table:

1. Create a new Vaadin project named *my-first-table* using your IDE.

2. Edit your `UI` class to match the following code snippet:

```
public class MyFirstTableUI extends UI {

  protected void init(VaadinRequest request) {
    final VerticalLayout layout = new VerticalLayout();
    layout.setMargin(true);
    setContent(layout);
  }
}
```

3. Now, add the actual code for the table shown as follows:

```
public class MyFirstTableUI extends UI {

    protected void init(VaadinRequest request) {

        // ...

        Table table = new Table();

        table.addContainerProperty("Column 1", String.class,
            "(default 1)");
        table.addContainerProperty("Column 2", String.class,
            "(default 2)");

        table.addItem(new Object[] { "Hi", "There" }, "item ID 1");
```

```
      table.addItem(new Object[] { "Well", "Hello!" }, "item ID
         2");
      table.addItem();

      layout.addComponent(table);
   }
}
```

4. Run it!

What just happened?

First of all, here is a screenshot of the table:

Let's cut the code up. You must create a `Table` instance as expected:

```
Table table = new Table();
```

Then, you must add columns:

```
table.addContainerProperty("Column 1", String.class, "(default 1)");
table.addContainerProperty("Column 2", String.class, "(default 2)");
```

We are adding two columns; each one will store a String value. If no value is specified for a column in some row, **(default 1)** and **(default 2)**, will be displayed on the table.

Do you remember *Chapter 2, Using Input Components and Forms – Time to Listen to Users*, where we discussed about properties, items, and containers? The addContainerProperty method seems to be adding properties to some container. That's right, that's what's happening here. Every Vaadin table is a container itself (in the Java sense), so we can add properties and items to it.

 A table uses a container behind the scenes to provide access to the data it should show. By default a Table is backed by an IndexedContainer, but you can change this using the setContainerDataSource method.

Adding properties to a table means the same as adding columns to a table. Note that we are adding properties to a Container, not to an Item, because we are defining columns, not the actual row values.

 Remember that Property stores a type and a value. An Item takes properties and gives them a name (property ID), so an Item is like a row, in the context of a table. A Container, takes items and in the same way, gives them a name (item ID). In this sense Table is like a frontend for a Container.

Once we have our columns ready, we can start adding rows, or more precisely, items as shown in the following code snippet:

```
table.addItem(new Object[] { "Hi", "There" }, "item ID 1");
table.addItem(new Object[] { "Well", "Hello!" }, "item ID 2");
table.addItem();
```

The first parameter is an array with the property values for the new row (or item). The array contains the property values in the same order as the columns were added.

If we are adding items, can we use the Vaadin data model explicitly to add these items? Yes, we can. For example, we could have added the first row using this code:

```
// add a new Item ready for setting property values
Item item1 = table.addItem("item ID 1");

// get the properties (one property per column)
```

```
Property column1 = item1.getItemProperty("Column 1");
Property column2 = item1.getItemProperty("Column 2");

// set the value for each property (or column)
column1.setValue("Hi");
column2.setValue("There");
```

> What are item ID 1 and item ID 2? These are arbitrary strings used to uniquely identify the items inside the container (table). Note that, you can pass any type for an item ID, not only String. If we have a reference to the container, we can get an Item from the item ID:
>
> ```
> Container container = table.getContainerDataSource();
> Item item1 = container.getItem("item ID 1");
> ```
>
> Or even more straightforward:
>
> ```
> table.getItem("Item ID 1");
> ```

Maybe you are wondering the reason to use the Property and Item interfaces instead of the quick and convenient methods to add rows to a table using arrays. Vaadin's data model allows you to use the standard interfaces to pass data to the UI components. No matter what UI component it is about, you can use the same data interfaces to display your data.

> A table can be attached to any container. For example, Vaadin comes with an SQLContainer implementation to handle relational data from SQL databases. If you have developed a nice table that displays data using SQLContainer, and at some point you need to switch to another persistent technology, you could write your own container, or use one of the containers available in the Vaadin directory (https://vaadin.com/directory) to communicate with your new datasource without changing the table implementation.

As you can see, the previous example adds an Item interface without any value for its properties:

```
table.addItem();
```

In this case, table will add a new Item interface with all the properties (columns) using the default values configured when we defined the columns. We could use the returned Item to set its property values, but we are not doing so just to see how the default values are rendered on the table.

Headers

What if we want to change the header of a column at runtime? This couldn't be more easier:

```
table.setColumnHeader("Column 1", "There you have, a new header");
```

In the preceding line of code, the first parameter is the property ID for the column, and guess what! The second parameter is the new header text. You can change all headers with a single call:

```
table.setColumnHeaders(new String[] {"Header 1", "Header 2"});
```

Are you interested in getting an array with the current column headers? There you go:

```
String[] columnHeaders = table.getColumnHeaders();
```

Maybe just the header for one particular column:

```
String columnHeader = table.getColumnHeader("Column 1");
```

You must provide the property ID of the desired column in the previous call.

Would you like to build a table with no header at all? Ok, that's easy:

```
table.setColumnHeaderMode(ColumnHeaderMode.HIDDEN);
```

Hey wait! That was indeed easy but kind of obscure though. That's right. `ColumnHeaderMode` is an enumeration that allows you to control what's going to be shown on the headers. Here you have a brief explanation of the available enum values:

Enum value	Description	Example
HIDDEN	No headers are shown.	Hi / There / Well / Hello! / (default 1) / (default 2)
ID	Property ID is used as header. If you call something like: `table. setColumnHeader("Column 1", "You won't see this text");` The column will still show the property ID as header (**COLUMN 1**).	COLUMN 1 / COLUMN 2 / Hi / There / Well / Hello! / (default 1) / (default 2)

Enum value	Description	Example
EXPLICIT	Headers must be explicitly specified. If a header is not specified, no text will be rendered.	Hi — There Well — Hello! (default 1) — (default 2)
EXPLICIT_DEFAULTS_ID	Headers can be explicitly specified, but if a header is not specified, the property ID is used. If you call something like: `table.setColumnHeader("Column 1", "Explicit header");` The column will show the new header.	EXPLICIT HEADER — COLUMN 2 Hi — There Well — Hello! (default 1) — (default 2)

Clicking on headers

You can listen to clicks on headers. Just add a `HeaderClickLister` method and put your custom code inside the `headerClick` method. For example, if you want to show a notification every time the user clicks on a header, you can do this:

```
table.addHeaderClickListener(new HeaderClickListener() {

  public void headerClick(HeaderClickEvent event) {
    Notification.show("Header clicked: " + event.getPropertyId());
  }

});
```

 Note that you can sort the rows by clicking on column headers even if you add a `HeaderClickListener` method. You can disable this sorting behavior by calling `table.setSortDisabled(true);`

Footers

Footers are the best place to show totals or any data related to columns. They are placed at the bottom of each table column. To show footers you have to make them visible by using the following:

```
table.setFooterVisible(true);
```

Then, you can set the footer using the `setColumnFooter` method:

```
table.setColumnFooter("Column 1", "Footer 1");
```

Clicking on footers

Similar to headers, you can add click listeners to the footers. The following code will show a notification every time the user clicks on the footer:

```
table.addFooterClickListener(new FooterClickListener() {

  public void footerClick(FooterClickEvent event) {
    Notification.show("Footer clicked: " + event.getPropertyId());
  }

});
```

Boxwords game

In this section we are going to develop a simple board game using the versatile `Table` component. **Boxwords** is a simple yet intriguing game, whose aim is to obtain the highest score by placing random letters in a grid. The player starts with an empty grid of twenty-five empty squares (5 x 5). At each turn, the application will show a random letter that the player must place in some empty square trying to form words of two or more letters either, vertically or horizontally. When the grid is full, the application will add up the score using a dictionary. The player will gain one point per letter of each correct word. Here is a screenshot of the finished application:

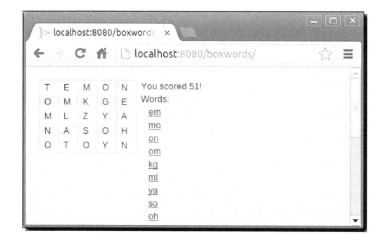

Time for action – implementing the game UI

We are ready to implement the UI part of the game. We will code everything in five methods: init (to initialize and wire up all the UI components), itemClick (to handle the clicks the user makes on the table), nextTurn (to update the UI on each turn), gameOver (to show the results when the game finishes), and getWords (that will return a collection with the correct words in the table). The steps for implementing the UI part of the game are as follows:

1. First step as always is to create a new Vaadin project. We are using *boxwords* for the name of the project.

2. Browse the book's source code and copy the Dictionary and Game classes and paste them beside your BoxwordsUI class. These classes implement the business logic for our game.

3. Open your UI class (BoxwordsUI in this example) and add the following members:

```
public class BoxwordsUI extends UI {

    private Game game = new Game(5);

    private Table table = new Table();
    private VerticalLayout messagesLayout = new VerticalLayout();
    private Label currentLetter = new Label("",
        ContentMode.HTML);

    protected void init(VaadinRequest request) { }

    public void itemClick(ItemClickEvent event) { }

    private void nextTurn() { }

    private void gameOver() { }

    private Collection<String> getWords() {
        return null;
    }

}
```

4. We have a game of five rows and five columns, a `table` to represent the grid, and a `VerticalLayout` (messagesLayout) that will contain a `Label` (currentLetter) to show the letter to place in the grid. In a further step, we will add the correct words found to the `messagesLayout` component. Let's set up all these components in our `init` method. Add the highlighted code (note that the class now implements `ItemClickListener`):

```
public class BoxwordsUI extends UI implements ItemClickListener
    {

    // ...

    protected void init(VaadinRequest request) {
      // init main layout
      HorizontalLayout layout = new HorizontalLayout();
      layout.setMargin(true);
      layout.setSpacing(true);
      setContent(layout);

      // init the table
      table.setPageLength(0);
      table.setColumnHeaderMode(ColumnHeaderMode.HIDDEN);
      table.addItemClickListener(this);

      for (int column = 0; column < game.getSize(); column++) {
        table.addContainerProperty(column, String.class, ".");
      }

      for (int row = 0; row < game.getSize(); row++) {
        table.addItem(row);
      }

      layout.addComponent(table);

      // init the components for showing the next letter and results
      messagesLayout.addComponent(currentLetter);
      layout.addComponent(messagesLayout);

      nextTurn();
    }
  }
```

5. At this point you can compile, and run the application. Do it.

What just happened?

This is how the application looks so far:

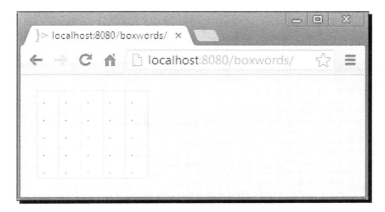

You can figure out the intention of most of the code. The only missing thing here is the line:

```
table.setPageLength(0);
```

Page length

The best way to understand what page length means, is to try using other values. If we use `table.setPageLength(2)` this would be rendered:

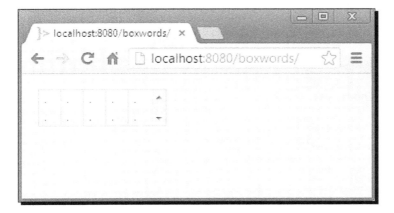

The page length tells the table how many rows to show. If we say *show zero rows*, the table will show all the rows with no scroll bars, and that's exactly what we want for our game.

Selecting items in tables

Tables can listen to clicks on rows. What you need to do is to add an `ItemClickListener` method to the table:

```
table.addItemClickListener(this);
```

Because we are passing a reference to our `UI` class (`this`), we must implement `ItemClickListener` in our `BoxwordsUI` class:

```
public class BoxwordsUI extends UI implements ItemClickListener {
  public void itemClick(ItemClickEvent event) { }
}
```

The `itemClick` method will be called every time the user clicks on a table row. Let's add that behavior right away.

Time for action – listening to clicks

Following are the steps to add the corresponding UI logic for the table clicking part:

1. Implement the `itemClick` method as follows:

    ```
    BoxwordsUI extends UI implements ItemClickListener {

      // ...

      public void itemClick(ItemClickEvent event) {
        Property property = event.getItem().getItemProperty(
          event.getPropertyId());

        if (".".equals(property.getValue())) {
          property.setValue(game.getCurrentLetter());
          nextTurn();

        } else {
          Notification.show("You must select an empty cell.");
        }
      }

      // ...

    }
    ```

2. Run the application and perform some clicks on the table.

What just happened?

The `event` variable gives us all we need to know about the performed click. We are using an `ItemClickListener`, right? This means that our method will be called every time the user clicks on an `Item`, and an `Item` is a row. But we need to know not only the row, but also the column. More precisely, we need the exact cell, and for a table, a cell is the same as a `Property`. Let's see how we can get the `Property`.

The `ItemClickEvent` class, has a method, that returns the `Item` which the user has clicked on:

```
Item clickedItem = event.getItem();
```

Good, we got the `Item` (row). But remember that an `Item` groups many properties each one with a property ID. We can get the property ID that the user clicked on by using:

```
Object clickedPropertyId = event.getPropertyId();
```

Nice. We have all that we need. We have the `Item` and the property ID. Now we are able to get the property itself:

```
Property property = clickedItem.getItemProperty(clickedPropertyId);
```

In our "boxwords" application we are combining everything in one sentence:

```
Property property = event.getItem().getItemProperty(
    event.getPropertyId());
```

At last! We have that elusive `Property`. All we have to do is to check if the current value of that property is a period character. If so, that means that the cell is empty and we can set the current letter as its value, otherwise, we show an appropriate message:

```
if (".".equals(property.getValue())) {
  property.setValue(game.getCurrentLetter());
  nextTurn();

} else {
  Notification.show("You must select an empty cell.");
}
```

Reading data from tables

Data in a table is managed through the `Container` interface. If you have an `Item` ID you can look for the `Item` itself and get all its properties. If you have a property, you can get its value. Let's use these concepts to implement the rest of the Boxwords game.

Time for action – finishing the game

Following are the steps to complete our game:

1. The `nextTurn` method checks if the game is over. If so, it will delegate control to the `gameOver` method, or else, it will generate the next random letter (by calling the `game.nextLetter()` method) and will update the label showing the new letter. As you have seen in previous snippets, this method is called every time the user clicks on an empty cell. Here is the implementation:

```java
public class BoxwordsUI extends UI implements ItemClickListener {

  // ...

  private void nextTurn() {
    if (game.over()) {
      gameOver();

    } else {
      currentLetter.setValue("Next letter: "
        + game.nextLetter());
    }
  }

  // ...

}
```

2. The `gameOver` method updates the UI to show the score and correct words. For each word, we include a link to the corresponding Merriam-Webster dictionary definition by using an HTML tag. Here is the implementation:

```java
public class BoxwordsUI extends UI implements ItemClickListener {

  // ...

  private void gameOver() {
    Collection<String> words = getWords();

    currentLetter.setValue("You scored "
      + game.getScore(words) + "!");

    messagesLayout.addComponent(new Label("Words:"));

    for (String word : words) {
```

```
        String link = "http://www.merriam-
        webster.com/dictionary/"
        + word.toLowerCase();
        // The following is not a good implementation.
        // Next chapter we will see how to get rid of this ugly
        // HTML.
        String anchor = "<a href='" + link
          + "' target='_blank' style='margin-left: 10px;'>"
          + word.toLowerCase() + "</a>";

        messagesLayout
          .addComponent(new Label(anchor, ContentMode.HTML));
      }
    }

    // ...

  }
```

3. Finally, the `getWords` method used in the previous `gameOver` method, builds strings with the data in the table and returns a `Collection` with all the correct words:

```
public class BoxwordsUI extends UI implements ItemClickListener {

// ...

  private Collection<String> getWords() {
    ArrayList<String> words = new ArrayList<String>();

    for (int row = 0; row < game.getSize(); row++) {
      String line = "";

      for (int column = 0; column < game.getSize(); column++) {
        line += table.getItem(row).
          getItemProperty(column).getValue();
      }

      words.addAll(game.getWords(line));
    }

    for (int column = 0; column < game.getSize(); column++) {
      String line = "";

      for (int row = 0; row < game.getSize(); row++) {
        line += table.getItem(row).
```

```
                getItemProperty(column).getValue();
        }

        words.addAll(game.getWords(line));
    }

    return words;
}

}
```

4. That's it. Now you can try to beat my score.

What just happened?

Hopefully, you would be able to figure out what all the previous code does. Let's review only the part that reads the content of the table. The `getWords` method contains two `for` loops. The first checks for words in rows, while the second checks for words in columns. What we are doing is iterating over the grid, getting the letter in each cell, or property, and concatenating them to get the string representing the entire row or column. Take a closer look at the body of the inner loop:

```
line += table.getItem(row).
   getItemProperty(column).getValue();
```

First we get the corresponding row. At this point you immediately think of an `Item`, right? I hope so. Getting the row is easy:

```
table.getItem(row);
```

Once we have the row, we get the column, or property:

```
table.getItem(row).getItemProperty(column);
```

Finally, we call the `getValue()` method to get the actual value in the cell.

Editable tables

Vaadin has a really cool feature that allows us to implement editable tables lightning fast. Let's say we have a table like this:

```
Table table = new Table();
table.setPageLength(0);

table.addContainerProperty("String", String.class, "");
table.addContainerProperty("Boolean", Boolean.class, false);
```

```
table.addContainerProperty("Date", Date.class, null);

table.addItem();
table.addItem();
table.addItem();
```

That is a simple table with three columns, each one storing properties of `String`, `Boolean`, and `Date` types. We have added three rows to it. This table will be rendered as follows:

Nothing's new so far. I said that it is lightning fast to create an editable table because it really is:

```
table.setEditable(true);
```

Take a look at the nice input components being automatically generated for us shown as follows:

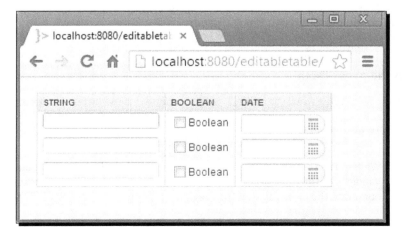

Besides `String`, `Boolean`, and `Date` types, an editable table also renders `Item` types. Suppose we have a `User` class as follows:

```
public class User {

  private String login;

  private String password;

  // ... getters and setters here ...

}
```

So we can create a `User` as shown:

```
User user = new User();
user.setLogin("mylogin");
user.setPassword("mypassword");
```

Now we can build an Item using the cool `BeanItem` class:

```
BeanItem<User> item = new BeanItem<User>(user);
```

> `BeanItem` uses the Java reflection API to create all the properties for a Java bean. Basically, `BeanItem` iterates over all the getters of the bean and creates a `MethodProperty` instance for each one. A `MethodProperty` is a special `Property` that can be attached to a bean and a Java getter. There's no magic, just the great combination of Java introspection capabilities, and Vaadin's data model.

Right now, `Item` has two properties: `login` and `password`. What we want to do is to add a column, not of type `String`, nor `Boolean`, nor `Date`, but of type `Item`. First we need to add the corresponding property to the container:

```
table.addContainerProperty("Item", Item.class, null);
```

Now we can add a row like this:

```
table.addItem(new Object[] { "", true, new Date(), item }, 4);
```

Note that we are adding all the previous properties and the new `item` hosting our `user`.

> We are using 4 as item ID, because we have already added three default items. Vaadin will use an `IndexedContainer` method that will automatically numerate the items, so that the previously added items have IDs 1, 2, and 3.

Take a look at how Vaadin will render the table:

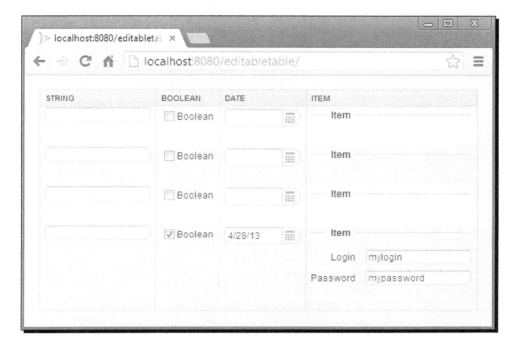

A form with all needed properties is created and rendered on the last column.

When we added the property for the **ITEM** column, we specified `null` as the default value, that's why, the first three rows are not showing a form. Those items have no idea of what kind of `Item` to render. If our goal had been to show empty user forms at each row, we could have added the container property using the following line:

```
table.addContainerProperty("Item", Item.class,
    new BeanItem<User>(new User()));
```

Table field factories

An editable `Table` delegates field creation to a `TableFieldFactory` instance. By default, a table uses a `DefaultFieldFactory` instance to do the job, but we can set our own `TableFieldFactory`.

Time for action – using a custom field factory

We are going to implement an editable table with two columns: **Login** and **Password**. We are very concerned about users' privacy, security, confidentiality, and protection. We have to protect passwords against intruders watching our screen. Follow the given steps:

1. Create a new Vaadin project called *fieldfactory*.

2. Now create a table with the two required properties and some testing rows:

```
public class FieldfactoryUI extends UI {

    @Override
    protected void init(VaadinRequest request) {
        final VerticalLayout layout = new VerticalLayout();
        layout.setMargin(true);
        setContent(layout);

        Table table = new Table("Users");
        table.setPageLength(0);
        table.setEditable(true);
        table.addContainerProperty("Login", String.class, "");
        table.addContainerProperty("Password", String.class, "");

        table.addItem();
        table.addItem();
        table.addItem();

        layout.addComponent(table);
    }
}
```

3. Running the application and typing in the text fields will render something as shown in the following screenshot:

4. Let's improve privacy. First, create a new class `UserFieldFactory`:

```
public class UserFieldFactory {
}
```

5. Let this class implement `TableFieldFactory`:

```
public class UserFieldFactory implements TableFieldFactory {

    @Override
    public Field<?> createField(Container container, Object
        itemId, Object propertyId, Component uiContext) {

        return null;
    }
}
```

6. As you could guess, the editable table will delegate the creation of the fields to the `createField` method. You have a reference to the container where the property belongs, the `itemID` (row), the `propertyID`, and a `context` representing the UI component where the field will be added. We can use the property ID to check if it is the **PASSWORD** column and return a more suitable field:

```
public class UserFieldFactory implements TableFieldFactory {
    @Override
    public Field<?> createField(Container container, Object
        itemId, Object propertyId, Component uiContext) {
        if ("Password".equals(propertyId)) {
            return new PasswordField();
        }

        return new TextField();
    }
}
```

7. Our factory is ready. Now we can use it in our table:

```
public class FieldfactoryUI extends UI {

    @Override
    protected void init(VaadinRequest request) {

        // ...
        table.setTableFieldFactory(new UserFieldFactory());
    }
}
```

8. Run and test the now highly secure application.

What just happened?

We are using our custom `TableFieldFactory` method to build all the fields for our editable table. For the **PASSWORD** column we are using the `PasswordField` method which replaces the typed characters:

Note, how we added a caption when we created the table:

```
Table table = new Table("Users");
```

 You can add Vaadin UI components directly to a `Table`.

You can add the following properties to a table:

```
table.addContainerProperty("Text fields",
    TextField.class, null);
table.addContainerProperty("Check boxes",
    CheckBox.class, null);
```

We have added two properties of type `TextField` and `CheckBox`. We can add a row showing the UI components using this line of code:

```
table.addItem(new Object[] { new TextField(),
    new CheckBox() }, 1);
```

The table will be rendered like this:

Understanding generated columns

Sometimes you need to calculate the content of one column based on the content of other columns. Generated columns are just great for accomplishing that. Suppose you have a table with two `Integer` columns:

```
Table table = new Table();
table.addContainerProperty("A", Integer.class, 0);
table.addContainerProperty("B", Integer.class, 0);
```

You want a third column with the sum of the previous columns. Here is the code to do that:

```
table.addGeneratedColumn("A + B", new ColumnGenerator() {
  @Override
  public Object generateCell(Table source, Object itemId,
      Object columnId) {
    Integer a = (Integer) source.getItem(itemId)
        .getItemProperty("A").getValue();

    Integer b = (Integer) source.getItem(itemId)
        .getItemProperty("B").getValue();
    return a + b;
  }
});
```

A column generator must implement the `generateCell` method that returns the value or the UI component to render on the cell. Here we are returning the calculated value, but we could have returned any UI component such as a `Label`:

```
table.addGeneratedColumn("A + B", new ColumnGenerator() {
    // ...
    return new Label("" + (a + b));
  }
});
```

This is a screenshot of the table:

We can format cells by overriding the `formatPropertyValue` method of `Table`. For example, suppose we want negative numbers to be rendered differently, that is, instead of showing **-5**, we want to show 5 in brackets, like **(5)**. The following is one way of accomplishing this:

```
Table table = new Table() {
  @Override
  protected String formatPropertyValue(Object rowId,
    Object colId, Property<?> property) {
    Integer n = (Integer) property.getValue();

    if (n < 0) {
      return "(" + (-n) + ")";
    }

    return "" + n;
  }
};
```

That will make our previous example look as shown in the following screenshot:

Collapsing and reordering columns

You can allow users to hide or show columns at runtime. All you have to do is to enable column collapsing:

```
table.setColumnCollapsingAllowed(true);
```

That will render a little menu to play with columns' visibility as shown in the next screenshot:

If you want to disable column collapsing for a certain column, you can do something similar to the following code snippet:

```
table.setColumnCollapsible("A + B", false);
```

You have to call `table.setColumnCollapsingAllowed(true);` when you want some columns to be noncollapsible. If you don't make this call, the menu showing the columns won't be rendered. You can use the `setColumnCollapsed` method to programmatically collapse a column. For example, if we wanted to collapse the A column of our previous example, we could do this by calling:

```
table.setColumnCollapsed("A", true);
```

Have a go hero – activate column reordering powers

Users can reorder the columns in tables. Just enable that feature:

```
table.setColumnReorderingAllowed(true);
```

Try modifying any example of this chapter by adding the previous line of code, run the application, and drag the table's headers.

Pop quiz – mastering tables

Here you go with the quiz to make sure you didn't lose anything:

Q1. Which interface does `Table` implement?

1. `Item`.
2. `Array`.
3. `Container`.

Q2. You can add a table column using the method:

1. `addContainerColumn`.
2. `addColumn`.
3. `addContainerProperty`.
4. `addColumnProperty`.

Q3. You can add a table row using the method:

1. `addItem`.
2. `addRow`.
3. `addContainerItem`.
4. `addContainerRow`.

Q4. Which line will add footer to the column ID `column1`:

1. `table.getColumn("column1").setColumnFooter("text");`
2. `table.getColumnFooter("column1").setValue("text");`
3. `table.setColumnFooter("column1", "text);`
4. `table.setFooter("column1", "text");`

Q5. To handle clicks on a `Table` you must add a:

1. `PropertyClickListener`.
2. `ItemClickListener`.
3. `ClickListener`.
4. `RowClickListener`.

Q6. If you want to hide the header of a table, you can call:

1. `table.setColumnHeaderMode(ColumnHeaderMode.HIDDEN);`

2. `table.setColumnHeaderVisible(false);`

Q7. `DefaultFieldFactory` is used by editable tables to automatically render fields of types:

1. `String` and `Boolean`.

2. `String, Boolean,` and `Date`.

3. `String, Boolean, Date,` and `Property`.

4. `String, Boolean, Date,` and `Item`.

Summary

Take a look at what we have covered in this chapter:

- We learned how to add columns and rows to tables.

- We learned that tables handle columns as properties and rows as items.

- We learned how to add headers and footers, and respond to clicks on them.

- We used Vaadin's data model to get the data that a `Table` stores.

- We built editable tables and customized the generated components for their cells using the `TableFieldFactory` method and generated columns.

- We learned how to activate column collapsing and reordering for tables.

Now you have the understanding to efficiently use the `Table` component. In the next chapter we'll take a look at the several cool UI components. It's going to be a fast trip that will complete your understanding of Vaadin's out of the box UI components.

6
Adding More Components

Now that you have a strong knowledge base about Vaadin, you are able to use any component that fits your needs. This chapter will introduce you to several UI components that would be worthwhile to bear in mind when developing Vaadin applications with great user experience.

This chapter will cover the following topics:

- ◆ Trees
- ◆ Tree tables
- ◆ Progress indicators
- ◆ Icons
- ◆ Images, Flash, video, audio, and other web content
- ◆ Sliders
- ◆ Color picker
- ◆ File download
- ◆ Context menus
- ◆ Drag-and-drop

Are you ready to take a fast trip through rich components? Hope you are. This chapter will complete the full view of out-of-the-box Vaadin UI components.

Trees

Trees are used to display hierarchical data in a very easy to understand fashion.

Time for action – my first tree

Let's start coding right away! Follow these steps to create your first tree:

1. Create a new Vaadin project named **my-first-tree** using your IDE.

2. Implement your UI class like this one:

```
public class MyFirstTreeUI extends UI {

    protected void init(VaadinRequest request) {
        final VerticalLayout layout = new VerticalLayout();
        layout.setMargin(true);
        setContent(layout);

        Tree familyTree = new Tree();

        familyTree.addItem("Families");
        familyTree.addItem("The Jackson");
        familyTree.addItem("The Simpsons");
        familyTree.addItem("The Rothschilds");
        familyTree.addItem("The Hapsburgs");
        familyTree.addItem("The Addams");

        familyTree.setParent("The Jackson", "Families");
        familyTree.setParent("The Simpsons", "Families");
        familyTree.setParent("The Rothschilds", "Families");
        familyTree.setParent("The Hapsburgs", "Families");
        familyTree.setParent("The Addams", "Families");

        familyTree.setChildrenAllowed("The Jackson", false);
        familyTree.setChildrenAllowed("The Simpsons", false);
        familyTree.setChildrenAllowed("The Rothschilds", false);
        familyTree.setChildrenAllowed("The Hapsburgs", false);
        familyTree.setChildrenAllowed("The Addams", false);

        layout.addComponent(familyTree);
    }

}
```

3. Run the application.

What just happened?

This is the resulting tree:

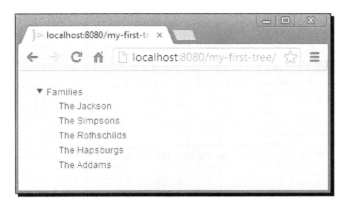

Most of the code is self-explanatory. We created a new instance of `Tree`, added some items (`addItem` method), established parent-child relationship between items (`setParent` method), and made some items to be leaves of the tree, so they won't have children (`setChildrenAllowed` method).

Alternatively, we could have used a `HierarchicalContainer`:

```
HierarchicalContainer container =
    new HierarchicalContainer();
container.addItem("Dad");
container.addItem("Sonny");
container.setParent("Sonny", "Dad");

familyTree.setContainerDataSource(container);
```

The similarity in the API used to add items and set parent-child relationships is not mere coincidence. `HierarchicalContainer` and `Tree` both implement the `Container.Hierarchical` interface. Now you can see the light.

Tree events

There are several listeners that you can add to a Tree. We are not covering all of them here, only some of the more relevant ones. The first one is about clicking on the items. How can you listen to clicks on items? You might have guessed:

```
familyTree.addItemClickListener(new ItemClickListener() {
  @Override
  public void itemClick(ItemClickEvent event) {
    Notification.show(event.getItemId() + " clicked.");
  }
});
```

Several Vaadin UI components use exactly the same listener.

There are two additional events that could be of interest when dealing with trees. The user can expand or collapse a node (if the node is allowed to have children), well, listening to these events is also pretty straightforward:

```
familyTree.addExpandListener(new ExpandListener() {
  @Override
  public void nodeExpand(ExpandEvent event) {
    Notification.show(event.getItemId() + " expanded.");
  }
});

familyTree.addCollapseListener(new CollapseListener() {
  @Override
  public void nodeCollapse(CollapseEvent event) {
    Notification.show(event.getItemId() + " collapsed.");
  }
});
```

Tree tables

There's a component that allows you to fuse tables and trees' powers into one single flexible and handy entity (users will love it!): `TreeTable`.

This component is so cool that we can't miss playing with it. We are going to develop a nice application to visualize all the files in some server's directory. In order to do that, we need to implement a complex algorithm to recursively seek for the files in the hard drive. Next, we have to implement another intricate algorithm to establish all the relationships between files and folders. Then we need to... Just kidding again! Vaadin team has already done the work for us.

Time for action – a file browser

Follow these steps and see how easy it is to create a basic file browser with Vaadin:

1. Launch your IDE and create a new Vaadin project named **treetable**. Come on! Do it! Invest five minutes (maybe less) in this exercise.

2. Let's start with this empty layout:

```java
public class TreetableUI extends UI {

    protected void init(VaadinRequest request) {
        final VerticalLayout layout = new VerticalLayout();
        layout.setMargin(true);
        setContent(layout);
    }

}
```

3. We are implementing a file browser, so we need the root directory to be shown:

```java
public class TreetableUI extends UI {

    protected void init(VaadinRequest request) {

        // ...

        File folder = VaadinService.getCurrent().getBaseDirectory();
    }

}
```

 VaadinService.getCurrent().getBaseDirectory() returns a File instance pointing to the directory where the application has been deployed. You can use another location if you want. Just make sure that the process running the application has permission to access the location. For example, if you are using Linux, you could change the folder instance to this:

```java
File folder = new File("/usr/local");
```

4. Now, we need a `Hierarchical` container. Any volunteers? `FilesystemContainer` raises its hand:

```
public class TreetableUI extends UI {

  protected void init(VaadinRequest request) {

    // ...

    File folder = VaadinService.getCurrent().getBaseDirectory();
    FilesystemContainer container =
      new FilesystemContainer(folder);

  }

}
```

5. Finally, we can add a `TreeTable` component and connect it to our container:

```
public class TreetableUI extends UI {

  protected void init(VaadinRequest request) {

    // ...

    TreeTable treeTable = new TreeTable();
    treeTable.setContainerDataSource(container);
    treeTable.setSizeFull();

    layout.addComponent(treeTable);
  }

}
```

6. Check it out. Deploy and test your application.

What just happened?

Five lines of code (we are not counting layout and related stuff because of marketing reasons) and we get this cool tree table:

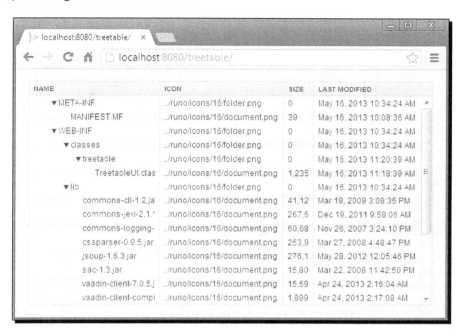

`TreeTable` extends `Table` and implements `Container.Hierarchical`. That's where the component gets all of its powers from. We are using a hierarchical container (`FilesystemContainer`) to delegate all the logic of getting files from the hard drive as items.

You can add items by hand using the `Hierarchical` interface and the `Table` methods. Let's see how. Tables have columns. Columns are properties. Therefore, we must add properties:

```
treeTable.addContainerProperty("Family", String.class, "");
treeTable.addContainerProperty("Members", Integer.class, null);
```

Now, we can add items containing values for the previous properties:

```
treeTable.addItem(new Object[] {"Families", null}, 0);
treeTable.addItem(new Object[] {"The Simpsons", 5}, 1);
treeTable.addItem(new Object[] {"The Addams", 8}, 2);
```

0, 1, and 2 are the items' IDs. So far, the code looks just like a regular `Table`: We defined columns and we added rows. Now, here comes the tree part. We can create parent-child relationships between rows. We have rows 0, 1, and 2. Rows 1 and 2 are children of 0:

```
treeTable.setParent(1, 0);
treeTable.setParent(2, 0);
```

This `treeTable` will be rendered like this:

So basically, think of a `TreeTable` as a standard `Table` in which you can set parent-child relationships between rows.

 In the previous `TreeTable`, you can see that **The Simpsons** and **The Addams** items show the indicator or icon that allows the user to expand the item. These items actually don't have any children, so when clicking on the indicator, no items will be shown, of course. If you want to hide these indicators, the `setChildrenAllowed` method of the `Hierarchical` interface is your friend.

Have a go hero – use TreeTable or Tree interchangeably

Modify our file browser example to use `Tree` instead of `TreeTable`. You will need to change two lines of code (one of the lines is an `import` statement).

Progress indicators

Author: Let me introduce you to a friend. `ProgressIndicator`, *reader. Reader,* `ProgressIndicator`.

Author: Now that you know each other, let's work together.

ProgressIndicator: Cool, what's the task to do?

Author: Well, our awesome algorithm is taking too long and users are just leaving our state-of-the-art web application. So `ProgressIndicator`, we need your help to give the user some feedback about the progress of the process.

ProgressIndicator: Sure.

Author: Thank you sir. Take a look at our original application implementing this Java `Thread` performing our high-tech algorithm:

```
public class ProgressindicatorUI extends UI {

  private class HighTechAlgorithm extends Thread {
    public void run() {
      try {

        for (int i = 0; i < 10; i++) {
          sleep(1000);
        }

      } catch (InterruptedException e) {
        e.printStackTrace();
      }
    }
```

```
    }

    protected void init(VaadinRequest request) {
      final VerticalLayout layout = new VerticalLayout();
      layout.setMargin(true);
      setContent(layout);

      Button button = new Button("Start awesome algorithm");

      button.addClickListener(new Button.ClickListener() {
        public void buttonClick(ClickEvent event) {
          new HighTechAlgorithm().start();
        }
      });

      layout.addComponent(button);
    }

}
```

ProgressIndicator: Wow! That's an awesome algorithm.

Author: Thank you. It took us months to implement it. Anyways, we would like to add you, Mr. ProgressIndicator, to our layout, so you can tell the user how the progress of the algorithm is going. Is that OK for you?

ProgressIndicator: Sure. Let me place myself as a private member of your UI class.

Author: Of course, come in. And please add yourself to our main layout:

```
    public class ProgressindicatorUI extends UI {

      private ProgressIndicator mrProgressIndicator =
          new ProgressIndicator();

      // ...

      protected void init(VaadinRequest request) {

        // ...

        layout.addComponent(mrProgressIndicator);
      }
    }
```

ProgressIndicator: What a nice place. Really high-tech.

Author: Yeah, we painted it Vaadin color.

ProgressIndicator: My favorite color!

Author: Nice. For each iteration of our algorithm I will update you, OK?

ProgressIndicator: Yes please.

Author: Cool. You accept values in which range?

ProgressIndicator: Give me a `float` between 0 and 1.

Author: OK. There you go:

```
public class ProgressindicatorUI extends UI {

  // ...

  private class HighTechAlgorithm extends Thread {

    public void run() {
      try {

        for (int i = 1; i <= 10; i++) {
          sleep(1000);
          mrProgressIndicator.setValue(i * 0.1f);
        }

      } catch (InterruptedException e) {
        e.printStackTrace();
      }
    }

  }
}
```

ProgressIndicator: Thank you. I think I'm ready.

Author: Great! Let's run the app. Are you ready *reader*? You have been kind of quiet lately.

ProgressIndicator: Yeah. I think she/he might be overwhelmed by the high-tech algorithm.

Author: That's reasonable. Let's test our application:

ProgressIndicator: Cool. I'm working properly!

Author: Wonderful job `ProgressIndicator`. Thank you very much.

ProgressIndicator: My pleasure.

Icons

You know something that make applications look awesome? Images! Almost every UI component in Vaadin can render icons. Let's add some cool icons!

Time for action – adding icons

Follow these steps and see how icons beautify applications:

1. Create a new Vaadin project. We are using *icons* as project name.
2. Add some class level fields for the input components in your UI class:

```
public class IconsUI extends UI {

    private TextField tf = new TextField("Email");
    private ComboBox cb = new ComboBox("Type");
    private TextArea ta = new TextArea("Details");
```

```
private OptionGroup og = new OptionGroup("Priority");
private Button bt = new Button("Send");

// ...

}
```

3. We don't want to go out of shape with our Vaadin skills right? Add all the input components using your knowledge to a layout like this:

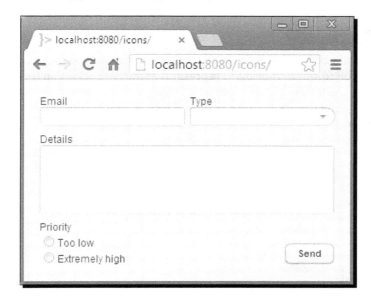

If you don't want to do this, you have two options: Copying the code from the book's source code, or adding all the components to a simple vertical layout.

4. Add the highlighted lines of code to the end of the init method:

```
public class IconsUI extends UI {

    // ...

    protected void init(VaadinRequest request) {
        tf.setIcon(new ClassResource("email.png"));
        cb.setIcon(new ClassResource("note.png"));
        ta.setIcon(new ClassResource("document.png"));
        bt.setIcon(new ClassResource("ok.png"));

        og.setItemIcon("Too low", new ClassResource("attention.png"));
```

```
        og.setItemIcon("Extremely high", new
          ClassResource("error.png"));
    }
}
```

5. Add the icon files into the same package `UI` class lives in. You can get the icons from the book's source code, or the `vaadin-themes-x.jar` (directory `VAADIN.themes/runo/icons/16`). You can put your own icons if you prefer.

6. Run and watch the difference.

What just happened?

Most Vaadin UI components have a `setIcon` method. This method expects a `Resource` object with the icon to set. A `Resource` represents some file such as an image, flash object, audio, and so on. Vaadin comes with several `Resource` implementations. Here we are using `ClassResource`, which looks for a file in your classpath. Take a look at the cool interface we have implemented:

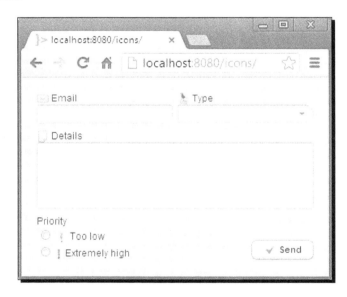

Images, Flash, video, audio, and other web content

In the previous section, we saw how to add an icon to a component through a `ClassResource` instance. A `Resource` represents web content such as images, flash files, audio files, video, or even an external web page.

Vaadin has two flavors of resources: Generic resources (implement `Resource`) and connector resources (implement `ConnectorResource`). A connector resource is specialized in the sense that it will connect to a resource through the Vaadin `Servlet` while a generic resource will bypass the `Servlet`.

We can choose from five `Resource` implementations:

Class	Description	Example
ExternalResource	Fetches a resource from a location specified by URL. The resource is fetched directly by the client.	`ExternalResource(` `"http://alejandrodu.com")`
ThemeResource	Vaadin applications can use a theme. A theme is a collection of web resources such as HTML templates, and CSS files. This implementation fetches the resource from the directory where the theme is located. We will cover Vaadin themes in the next chapter.	`ThemeResource(` `"common/icons/error.png")`
ClassResource	Fetches a resource located in the class path (besides `.class` files).	`new ClassResource(` `"globe.png")`
FileResource	Fetches a resource located anywhere in the server's file system.	`new FileResource(new` `File("C:/readme.txt"))`

StreamResource	Fetches a resource provided by a Java `InputStream`.	`StreamSource mySource =`
		`  new StreamSource() {`
		`    public InputStream`
		`getStream() {`
		`      // return custom`
		`InputStream`
		`    }`
		`};`
		
		`new StreamResource(`
		`mySource, "hello.txt");`

Once we have a `Resource`, we can use a UI component to visualize it. Not any component! Vaadin comes with specialized UI components to render several types of resources:

Class	Description
Image	Can you guess who can render images?
Flash	Guess who can render Flash objects.
Audio	Who can play audio?
Video	And guess who is responsible for video.
BrowserFrame	What about HTML frames?
Embedded	We can't use the same joke here. So, this class is for other web resources such as PDF, applets, or other multimedia content.

Let's summarize:

1. Choose a proper `Resource` implementation according to where the resource is located.

2. Next, select the best UI component according to the content type of the resource.

Time for action – render web content

Let's see that in action.

1. Create a new Vaadin project. We are using **resources** as project name.

2. Implement your UI class:

```
public class ResourcesUI extends UI {

  protected void init(VaadinRequest request) {
    final TabSheet sheets = new TabSheet();
    sheets.setSizeFull();
    setContent(sheets);

    Image imageFromTheme = new Image(null, new ThemeResource(
        "common/icons/error.png"));
    imageFromTheme.setSizeFull();

    Image imageFromClasspath = new Image(null, new
    ClassResource(
        "globe.png"));
    imageFromClasspath.setSizeFull();

    BrowserFrame frameFromURL = new BrowserFrame(null,
```

```
              new ExternalResource("http://alejandrodu.com"));
        frameFromURL.setSizeFull();

        BrowserFrame frameFromFileSystem = new BrowserFrame(null,
            new FileResource(new File("C:/readme.txt")));

        StreamSource mySource = new StreamSource() {
          public InputStream getStream() {
            return new InputStream() {

              private int size = 20;

              public int read() throws IOException {

                if (size-- > 0) {
                  return 'V'; // we are returning 20 V's.
                }

                return -1;
              }
            };
          }
        };

        BrowserFrame frameFromStream = new BrowserFrame(null,
            new StreamResource(mySource, "hello.txt"));

        Flash flashFromURL = new Flash(null, new ExternalResource(
            "http://www.youtube.com/v/ALgCDkZvzeY&hl=en_US&fs=1"));
        flashFromURL.setSizeFull();

        sheets.addTab(imageFromTheme, "Image from theme");
        sheets.addTab(imageFromClasspath, "image from classpath");
        sheets.addTab(frameFromURL, "Frame from URL");
        sheets.addTab(frameFromFileSystem, "Frame from file
        system");
        sheets.addTab(frameFromStream, "Frame from InputStream");
        sheets.addTab(flashFromURL, "Flash from URL");
    }
}
```

3. Long code. But it's not difficult. We are just covering almost everything about Vaadin resources in one example.

4. Run the application.

What just happened?

Let's study the case of the image from an InputStream. If you understand that, you can easily extrapolate the knowledge to understand the other cases. Here is a screenshot:

The aim is to show web content that is generated at runtime by the application. In this case we are generating plain text, but it could be any binary data representing some multimedia content. First, we need an Input stream that Vaadin will use to get the bytes of the content to render:

```
new InputStream() {

  private int size = 20;

  public int read() throws IOException {

    if (size-- > 0) {
      return 'V'; // we are returning 20 V's.
    }

    return -1;
  }
};
```

This anonymous InputStream will return 20 repeated characters. What Resource implementation must we use? We have an InputStream here, so we can't use ExternalResource, ThemeResource, ClassResource, or FileResource. The only alternative is StreamResource. This implementation expects a StreamResource. StreamSource implementation. StreamSource is an interface with one single method:

```
public interface StreamSource extends Serializable {
  public InputStream getStream();
}
```

As you can see, we must return an `InputStream`. So we just return the previous anonymous implementation:

```
StreamSource mySource = new StreamSource() {
  public InputStream getStream() {
    return new InputStream() {
      // ...
    };
  }
};
```

We can create a `StreamResource` now with this sentence:

```
new StreamResource(mySource, "hello.txt");
```

Now, we want to show this resource as what? Image? Flash? Frame? That last is correct! We can use a frame to show our resource. So we create a `BrowserFrame` instance and pass it the `StreamResource` we just created:

```
BrowserFrame frameFromStream = new BrowserFrame(null,
    new StreamResource(mySource, "hello.txt"));
```

Something similar happens with the rest of the resources we are displaying. Moreover, the other resources of the example are simpler, because we don't need to deal with `StreamSource` and `InputStream` implementations.

Sliders

A Slider is a component that allows the user to drag an indicator to select a value within a configurable range. The following code will create a slider to select a value between `0` and `100`:

```
Slider slider = new Slider("Drag the point");
slider.setMin(0.0);
slider.setMax(100.0);
```

We can set a value programmatically using the `setValue` method:

```
slider.setValue(30.0);
```

 If an out of the range value is set a `ValueOutOfBoundsException` is thrown.

This is how sliders look like:

Like many other input components, we can listen to value changes:

```
slider.addValueChangeListener(new ValueChangeListener() {
  public void valueChange(ValueChangeEvent event) {
    Notification.show("Attention! Slider value has changed to "
        + event.getProperty().getValue());
  }
});
```

Color picker

Vaadin includes a nice color selection component:

Have a go hero – experiment with ColorPicker

Add a `ColorPicker` component to some Vaadin application. Usage is pretty straightforward. Try creating an instance of `ColorPicker` and adding a `ColorChangeListener` to see how the color format is retrieved.

File download

In *Chapter 2, Using Input Components and Forms – Time to Listen to Users*, we learned how to upload files. Now we're going to learn how to download files. Let's say we have a PDF file and want users to download it by clicking a button. Doing it is quite easy. First a PDF file is a `Resource`, right? Suppose the file is in the classpath:

```
ClassResource resource = new ClassResource("enterprise-app.pdf");
```

We also need a `Button`:

```
Button button = new Button("Download the PDF");
button.setStyleName(BaseTheme.BUTTON_LINK);
```

 Use `button.setStyleName(BaseTheme.BUTTON_LINK)` to render the button like a standard link. Next chapter we'll learn more about styles.

The following two lines will make the rest of the job:

```
FileDownloader downloader = new FileDownloader(resource);
downloader.extend(button);
```

`FileDownloader` is an `Extension`. En `Extension` is an interface that allows adding functionality to a component. This particular extension starts a download when the extended component is clicked. Take a look at a screenshot of the extended button:

Context menus

A context menu appears when the user right-clicks some component. Vaadin supports context menus for `Table`, `Tree`, and `TreeTable`. Menu options are encapsulated using `Action` instances:

```
final Action action = new Action("Say hello");
```

To add actions and respond to them, we must add a `Handler`. A `Handler` is an interface with two methods:

```
public interface Handler extends Serializable {

  public Action[] getActions(Object target, Object sender);

  public void handleAction(Action action, Object sender,
      Object target);

}
```

`getActions` must return an array containing all the actions we want to show in our context menu. `handleAction` will be called when an action is performed (the user clicks a menu item). Here is an example implementation that shows a somewhat uncouth salutation:

```
table.addActionHandler(new Handler() {

  public void handleAction(Action action, Object sender,
      Object target) {
    Notification.show("Ok, here I go... Hello.");
  }

  public Action[] getActions(Object target, Object sender) {
    return new Action[] { action };
  }
});
```

Drag-and-drop

Drag-and-drop allows users to click a component, drag it through the screen, and drop it into another component. When the drop is performed the application state changes or some event is performed. Drag-and-drop adds functionality without showing additional buttons in the UI which reduces complexity and makes your applications more user-friendly.

Providing D&D fun in Vaadin applications is quite easy. There are two main concepts regarding drag-and-drop. The first is the component to be dragged (let's call it the transferable object). The second is the component where the dragged component will be dropped (let's call it the destiny object). Enabling drag-and-drop consists of enabling dragging in the transferable object and enabling dropping in the destiny object.

This snippet will enable dragging for the `button` instance:

```
DragAndDropWrapper draggable = new DragAndDropWrapper(button);
draggable.setDragStartMode(DragStartMode.WRAPPER);

layout.addComponent(draggable); // add it to some layout
```

We can wrap any UI component using a `DragAndDropWrapper` instance. Notice that we add the `draggable` instance instead of the `button` instance to the layout.

The user can now drag the `button` but can't drop it anywhere yet. Suppose we have a `destinyLayout` where the button can be dropped. We must enable dropping in the `destinyLayout`. We have to do two things. First we need to wrapper the `destinyLayout` into a `DragAndDropWrapper`:

```
DragAndDropWrapper destiny = new DragAndDropWrapper(
    destinyLayout);
layout.addComponent(destiny);
```

Note again that we added the `destiny` component instead of the `destinyLayout` to the `layout`. And second, we need to set a `DropHandler`:

```
destiny.setDropHandler(new DropHandler() {

  @Override
  public AcceptCriterion getAcceptCriterion() {
    return AcceptAll.get();
  }

  @Override
  public void drop(DragAndDropEvent event) {
    Notification.show("Dropped!");
  }
});
```

getAcceptCriterion must return an AcceptCriterion instance that indicates whether the drop method will be called or not for an specific transferable object. The drop method will be called when the user drops the component in the destiny object.

 Vaadin includes several AcceptCriterion implementations that are enough most of the time. In the previous example we are using AcceptAll, a singleton instance that accepts any component. To get more information about the available criteria implementations, take a look at the API documentation for AcceptCriterion at https://vaadin.com/api/.

Have a go hero – study a drag-and-drop example

We have a nice example showing some drag-and-drop features:

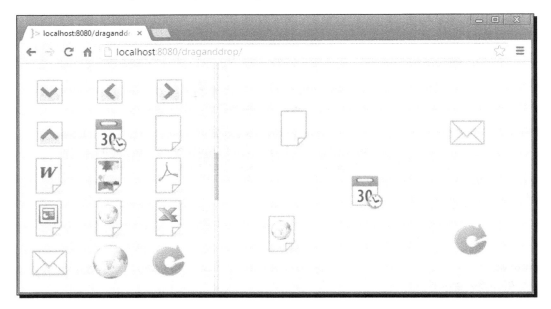

In this example, we have a GridLayout showing a variety of icons that can be dragged and dropped into the AbsoluteLayout on the right. Take a look at the draggable project and see how easy it is to implement this kind of behavior for your own applications.

Pop quiz – more components

Check your knowledge and make sure you are not missing something important:

Q1. Which container is more appropriate for a `Tree`?

1. `HierarchicalContainer`.
2. `TreeContainer`.
3. `BeanContainer`.

Q2. Which container is appropriate to handle files in the server's hard disk?

1. `ServerContainer`.
2. `HarddiskContainer`.
3. `FilesystemContainer`.

Q3. A `ClassResource` is used to fetch resources from:

1. The server's hard drive.
2. A custom stream of bytes.
3. The `classpath`.

Q4. If you want to add an icon to some component, which method would you call?

1. `addIcon(String filename)`.
2. `addIcon(Resource resource)`.
3. `setIcon(Resource resource)`.
4. `setIcon(String filename)`.

Q5. To render a `Resource` you can:

1. Add a `ResourceComponent`.
2. Call the method `setResource` of any UI component.
3. Add `Image`, `Video`, `Flash`, `Audio`, `BrowserFrame`, or `Embedded` components.

Q6. To enable drag-and-drop you must:

1. Turn drag-and-drop on in UI component.
2. Enable drag in a draggable component and enable drop in a destiny component.
3. Implement `Draggable` interface.

Summary

Phew! What a lot of new components! Take a look at what we have learned in this chapter:

- We learned how to use `Tree` by adding items and setting parent-child relationships between them.

- We learned that `TreeTable` is like a regular Table that allows us to establish parent-child relationships between rows.

- We learned (in a funny situation) how to work with `ProgressIndicator`.

- We (finally!) added some icons to our components.

- We learned how to incorporate any kind of web resources to our Vaadin applications using `Resource` implementations to get the resource and specific components (such as `Image`, `Flash`, and `BrowserFrame`) to render several types of resources.

- We learned how to use sliders and color pickers.

- We learned how to allow file downloading.

- We learned how to add context menus on trees and tables.

- We learned how to enable drag-and-drop and respond to dropping events on destiny components.

I'm glad to tell you that you are ready to take another step towards Vaadin expertise. Next chapters will explain customization at two levels: Themes and custom components. Do you want to master Vaadin? If so, I will see you in the next chapter.

7
Customizing UI Components – Time to Theme it

The example applications you have developed so far look really cool thanks to the out-of-the-box styles in Vaadin. However, you can dress your applications with your own style! Would you like to have a panel with a modern shadowing look? What about hovering effects for table rows? You can do all these things and more with Vaadin. CSS, and Sass enable Vaadin developers to customize the way components look on the browser by defining rules that change the styles used by the HTML tags being rendered. This chapter will teach you the basics of CSS and Sass and will show you how to style UI components by creating new Vaadin themes.

This chapter will cover the following topics:

◆ Vaadin themes
◆ CSS and Sass
◆ Firebug and Chrome inspector
◆ Styling labels
◆ Styling text fields
◆ Styling buttons
◆ Styling panels
◆ Styling menus
◆ Styling tables

It's time to theme it! With no more preambles, let's go ahead and start characterizing Vaadin applications by giving them their own styles.

Vaadin themes

A **Vaadin theme** is a set of resources (mainly HTML, CSS/Sass, and images) that define the styles to be used to render UI components. Vaadin ships with four ready to use themes. Let's see them in action.

Time for action – changing themes

Follow these steps to explore the different themes that come with Vaadin:

1. Open the example application named **themes** on your IDE.

2. Run the application. Pretty much the same as the previous examples. Actually, the same we are used to:

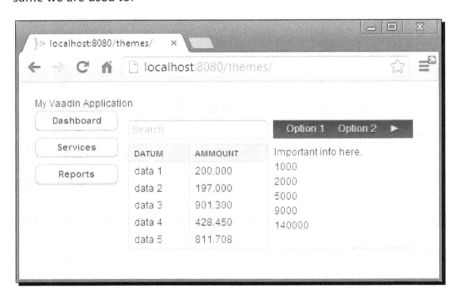

3. Edit the `ThemesUI` class to match the highlighted code:

```
@Theme("runo")
public class ThemesUI extends UI {

    // ...

    }
}
```

4. Run the application.

5. Aha! That's one small change for code, one giant leap for UI:

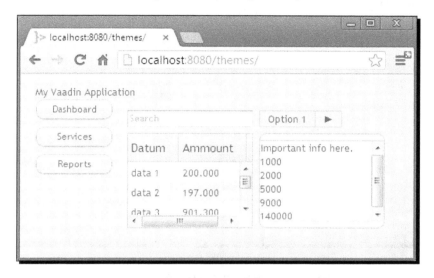

6. Now change the theme to `chameleon` and check it out:

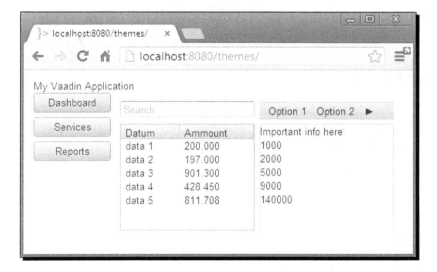

7. And one final theme, `liferay`:

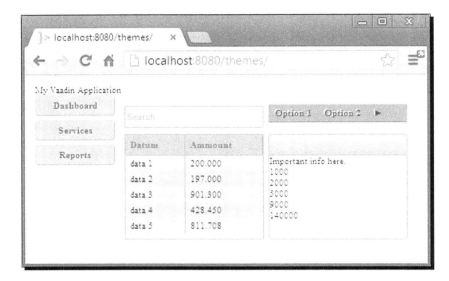

 Liferay is an open source enterprise portal. A portal implements most features common to websites, such as, user registration, authorization, community and collaboration. You can develop your own functionality by implementing portlets using Vaadin. For more information, consult JSR-286, the Java specification for portlets technology.

What just happened?

Changing the theme for your application is as easy as annotating your `UI` class:

```
@Theme("chameleon")
public class ThemesUI extends UI {

    // ...

}
```

The previous annotation will make Vaadin look for the `chameleon` directory in the `themes` path and use the contained resources to apply makeup for UI components. Before we learn where this path is and how to create new themes, we need to grasp a little bit of theory.

Introduction to CSS and Sass

You know your Vaadin UI components are ultimately rendered as HTML right? HTML is the language that browsers understand. But there is another kind of language that browsers also understand: CSS. **CSS** stands for **Cascading Style Sheets** and allows developers and web designers to specify the appearance of a web page in separate files. Suppose you have an HTML file `page.html`:

```
<html>
  <body>
    <h1>Hello</h1>

    <div>
      I'm a div :)
    </div>

  </body>
</html>
```

This page will be rendered like this:

With CSS, we can create a `.css` file to specify styling rules. Let's say we want to change the background and font colors of the body content. We can create a rule to do exactly that:

```
body {
    background-color: #555;
    color: #eef;
}
```

The previous rule stands for something like "for each body element in the HTML file, use `#555` as background color and `#eef` as font color".

#555 and #eef are colors expressed as the combination of red, green, and blue values, using a hexadecimal notation. A hexadecimal color is specified as #RRGGBB, where RR is the red value, GG is the green value, and BB is the blue value. In the previous example, #555 is an abbreviation for #555555, and #eef is an abbreviation for #eeeeff.

If we save this file with the name `mystyles.css` and add a head link in our HTML file to use it:

```html
<html>
  <head>
    <link href="mystyles.css" rel="stylesheet" type="text/css" />
  </head>

  <body>
    <h1>Hello</h1>

    <div>
      I'm a div :)
    </div>

  </body>
</html>
```

The page will look like this:

A CSS rule is specified using the following general syntax:

```
selector {property: value;}
```

The `selector` part answers the question: What HTML elements does the rule apply to? It could be `body`, `div`, `input`, or any other HTML tag. The `property: value` part defines the rule. There are properties such as `background-color`, `color` (to set the color of text), `font-family`, `font-size`, `margin` (to clear an area around an element), `border` (to specify the type of border), and a lot more.

The selector part not only allows you to select HTML tags, you could also select a custom group of elements or even a specific element. This is accomplished using the `class` and `id` attributes on the HTML tags respectively.

Every HTML element can specify a `class` attribute. For example, we can change our `div` element to specify a custom value for class:

```
<div class="cool-light-div">
  I'm a div :)
</div>
```

We can use this value to apply a CSS rule only to this particular element (in fact, to any element that includes the CSS class named `cool-light-div`). This is done by adding a dot before our CSS class name:

```
.cool-light-div {
  background-color: #eee;
  color: #333;
}
```

The rule will be applied to our `div` element:

We can also specify an id attribute for a HTML element:

```
<div id="my-div">
  I'm a div :)
</div>
```

In this case we will need to change the selector part of our CSS rule to this:

```
#my-div {
  background-color: #eee;
  color: #333;
}
```

Note the sharp sign used on the selector, this indicates that the rule will be applied to the HTML element defining the id my-div.

 We can't cover all CSS theory in this chapter. If you want to learn more about CSS, take a look at the learning resources at http://www.w3.org/Style/CSS/learning. Learning CSS is worthwhile if you are planning to create custom components or Vaadin themes.

All of the elements Vaadin render will have some particular value for the class attribute so you can use this value to modify certain elements. However, in Vaadin you won't use CSS directly but a powerful extension to CSS, **Syntactically Awesome Stylesheets** or **Sass**. You can use Sass by defining rules in .scss files and compiling them to generate standard CSS files that the browser can consume.

Variables

Sass allows you to define variables to avoid hard-coding values that are difficult to change. Suppose you have a cool background color and want to use it on several rules. With Sass, you can define a variable like this:

```
$cool-background: #336ea9;
```

Later, you can use the variable $cool-background:

```
.cool-div {
  background-color: $cool-background;
}
```

Nesting

With Sass, you can avoid repeating code by using nesting. For example:

```
.cool-div {
  background-color: #eee;
  color: #333;

  .otherdiv {
    margin: 20px;
  }
}
```

This will be compiled to:

```
.cool-div {
  background-color: #eee;
  color: #333;
}

.cool-div .otherdiv {
  margin: 20px;
}
```

Mixins

Sass mixins allows you to reuse whole chunks of CSS:

```
@mixin boxed {
  border: 1px solid #ccc;
}

.cool-div {
  background-color: #eee;
  color: #333;
  @include boxed;
}
```

The previous snippet will be compiled to:

```
.cool-div {
  background-color: #eee;
  color: #333;
  border: 1px solid #ccc;
}
```

You can give argument to mixins:

```
@mixin boxed($thickness) {
  border: $thickness solid #ccc;
}

.cool-div {
  background-color: #eee;
  color: #333;
  @include boxed(1px);
}
```

Sass is out of the scope of this book. However, Internet is full of tutorials, reference, and examples that you can read to gain more knowledge on this topic. For more information about Sass, visit http://sass-lang.com.

Introducing Firebug and Chrome inspector

At this point, you understand that your Vaadin UI components are rendered as HTML elements. Each element has a `class` attribute. If you know the value for this property, you can add Sass rules to it. Nice. However, how to know the value of this property? Most web browsers include developer tools to inspect the HTML being rendered. We are going to take a fast look at how to inspect HTML in Firefox and Chrome.

Firebug is a Firefox extension that allows you to edit, debug, and watch HTML, CSS, and JavaScript in any web page. You can install Firebug from http://getfirebug.com.

Chrome DevTools is the Chrome counterpart of Firebug. Chrome DevTools is bundled in Chrome.

 Internet Explorer ships with Developer Tools. However, we are not covering Developer Tools here. You can activate Developer Tools by pressing *F12*.

Time for action – inspecting HTML

Follow these steps to inspect the HTML generated by Vaadin:

1. Run the *themes* example application.
2. Browse to the application using Firefox or Chrome (make sure you have installed Firebug if using Firefox).
3. Right click on the **Dashboard** button and select **Inspect Element with Firebug** if you are in Firefox, or **Inspect element** if you are in Chrome.
4. Take a look at the actual HTML code Vaadin is generating for the button.

What just happened?

You just learned how to inspect HTML. If you look carefully, you can see several class values:

```
<div tabindex="0" role="button" class="v-button v-widget v-has-width"
    style="width: 100%;">

    <span class="v-button-wrap">
```

```
    <span class="v-button-caption">Dashboard</span>
  </span>

</div>
```

For example, the outer `div` element is using three CSS classes: `v-button`, `v-widget`, and `v-has-width`.

> If you don't use Firebug or Chrome DevTools, you can display the HTML of the current page of the browser by pressing *Ctrl + U*. However, if you do so, you won't see the current HTML that builds the UI. Instead, you will see mostly JavaScript. This is part of the JavaScript code that Vaadin uses to generate the HTML needed. By using Firebug or Chrome DevTools, we are looking at the current state of the HTML rendered on the browser, while the *Ctrl + U* option will show only the first snapshot of the HTML sent by the server when we first requested the page.

Creating new themes

Let's get started! It's time to create our first Vaadin theme.

Time for action – creating a new Vaadin theme

Follow these steps to create a new Vaadin theme:

1. Open the **themes** example application on your IDE.

2. Create a new `VAADIN/themes/cool/` folder besides your **WEB-INF** folder:

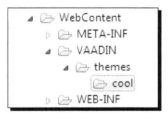

3. Create a new file `styles.scss` in the newly created directory and let your fingers type this into the new file:

```
@import "cool.scss";

.cool {
  @include cool;
}
```

4. Create a new file `cool.scss` in the newly created directory and allow your fingers to type this into the new file:

```
@import "../chameleon/chameleon.scss";

@mixin cool {
  @include chameleon;
}
```

5. Use the theme in `ThemesUI`:

```
@Theme("cool")
public class ThemesUI extends UI {

  // ...

}
```

6. Run the application and make sure that it's using the `chameleon` theme.

What just happened?

We've just created a new theme with the name `cool`. Configuring `@Theme("cool")` will make Vaadin search for a `cool` directory inside `VAADIN/themes/`. More precisely, Vaadin will load the file `VAADIN/themes/cool/styles.scss`.

The first line of `syles.scss` imports another file:

```
@import "cool.scss";
```

That means that the content of `cool.scss` will be available in `syles.scss`. Next, we define a new rule for elements with class cool:

```
.cool {
  @include cool;
}
```

Remember mixins? Well, `@include cool` is just including the rules in the `cool` mixing defined in `cool.scss`. Now, `cool.scss` imports another file:

```
@import "../chameleon/chameleon.scss";
```

This makes all the content of `chameleon.csss` available in `cool.scss`. Then we have the actual `mixin`:

```
@mixin cool {
  @include chameleon;
  /* We will insert our custom rules here */
}
```

Basically, we are extending the `chameleon` theme. This is too much coolness!

Styling labels

Let's apply all this vast knowledge we've just acquired to start shaping our style. Labels are kind of easy so we are starting with them.

Time for action – creating a new Vaadin theme

Follow these steps to change the way labels look:

1. Open the *themes* example application on your IDE.

2. Edit the `cool` mixin (in `cool.scss`) to include one rule for labels:

```
@mixin cool {
  @include chameleon;

  .v-label {
    color: #fff;
    background-color: #4455aa;
    font: 16px Verdana, Arial;
    padding: 5px;
    margin-bottom: 10px;
  }

}
```

3. Run the application.

What just happened?

Well, this happened:

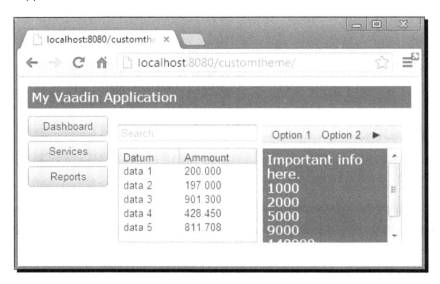

We defined a rule to be applied to labels. The CSS class `v-label` is automatically added to every label element.

> How to know which CSS classes are added by Vaadin? The fastest way to get this information is by inspecting the HTML in your browser. You can also find this information in the Book of Vaadin, the official Vaadin reference. For example, if you are interested in the CSS classes used for Label, you can take a look at (`https://vaadin.com/book/vaadin7/-/page/components.label.html`).

Adding CSS classes to components

In the previous section we created a rule to change the way every `Label` component was rendered. We had two labels in our application so both of them where changed. What if we want to change the style only for the title label? We can't keep using the `v-label` CSS class for our rule because it will change all the labels. We have to change the rule to something like this:

```
.page-header {
  color: #fff;
  background: #4455aa;
  font: 16px Verdana, Arial;
```

```
      padding: 5px;
      margin-bottom: 10px;
}
```

Instead of using v-label we use .page-header (note that the dot is required to define a rule for a CSS class). But Vaadin doesn't know anything about page-header. We must explicitly add the CSS class in our Java code:

```
Label title = new Label("My Vaadin Application");
title.addStyleName("page-header");
```

addStyleName will add the page-header CSS class to the title component. Take a look at the HTML Vaadin will render if we add the previous page-header CSS class:

```
<div class="v-label v-widget page-header v-label-page-header v-has-
width"
    style="width: 100%;">
        My Vaadin Application
</div>
```

As you can see, Vaadin adds page-header and v-label-page-header, this means that we could have defined our rule as:

```
.v-label-page-header {
  color: #fff;
  background: #4455aa;
  font: 16px Verdana, Arial;
  padding: 5px;
  margin-bottom: 10px;
}
```

When you add a style name to a component, Vaadin will add the corresponding CSS classes to all the child components. By using v-label-page-header, we can add a style name to only one component (for example headerLayout.addStyleName("page-header")) and define multiple individual CSS rules for each type of component.

All the four default Vaadin themes have a corresponding Java class containing static strings with the name of several CSS classes defined in the theme. These Java classes are Reindeer, Runo, ChameleonTheme, and LiferayTheme. All extend BaseTheme which in turn defines common styles. For example, you can make a Button component look like a regular link by adding the link CSS class. You can add this style by typing the name as a string:

```
button.addStyleName("link");
```

Or by using the corresponding constant defined in `BaseTheme`:

```
button.addStyleName(BaseTheme.BUTTON_LINK);
```

With the information you have up until now, you can design your own themes. The following sections will show you examples of custom styles for some of the most used Vaadin components.

Styling text fields

Text fields have the `v-textfield` CSS class. However, sometimes we need to do some tricks in order to accomplish our styling purposes. For example, if we want to make the text field have some rounded borders and a little icon inside the field, we could think of doing just this:

```
.v-textfield {
  border: 1px solid #4455aa;
  border-radius: 10px;
  -webkit-border-radius: 10px;
  -moz-border-radius: 10px;
  background:#FFFFFF url("search.png") no-repeat 5px 2px;
  padding-left: 22px;
}
```

That won't work when extending any of the default themes. The reason is that the themes are defining more specific rules for input elements. You can use Firebug or Chrome DevTools to inspect the element and see that the new rule is listed, but the theme selector comes first in the CSS order, so the extended theme rule has precedence. To change this, we need to override the rule for input elements:

```
input.v-textfield {

  /* ... */

}
```

But there are several input components and the default themes are defining rules for text input components. So we have to override the rule for *text* input components:

```
input.v-textfield[type=text] {

  /* ... */

}
```

The type=text chunk is an attribute selector. If you take a look at the actual HTML for a TextField component, you will see something like

```
<input type="text" ... >
```

type is an attribute. In CSS you can make a rule more specific by selecting a particular attribute value. In the previous example, we selected the text value for the type attribute.

Now, text fields will be rendered like this:

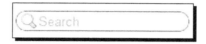

Styling buttons

Most of the time we will need two classes to style buttons: v-button and v-button-caption. Here is an example to change the color and size of buttons:

```
.v-button {
  color: #fff;
  background-color: #4455aa;
  border: 1px solid #4455aa;
  text-shadow:2px 2px 0px #474746;
  height: 50px;
  font-family:Trebuchet MS;
  font-weight: bold;
}
```

Styling panels

Panels are rendered like this:

```
<div class="v-panel ... " ... >

  <div class="v-panel-captionwrap" ... >

    <div class="v-panel-nocaption">
      <span>My caption</span>
    </div>
  </div>

  <div class="v-panel-content ..." ... >
```

```
      </div>

      <div class="v-panel-deco" ... >
      </div>

    </div>
```

Here is some CSS magic to make panels look like a post-it:

```css
    .v-panel {
      overflow: auto;
    }

    .v-panel-content {
      background: #ffee00;
      border: 0px #fff;
      padding: 10px;
      font-family: cursive, sans-serif;
    }

    .v-panel:before, .v-panel:after {
      z-index: -1;
      position: absolute;
      content: "";
      bottom: 15px;
      left: 10px;
      width: 50%;
      top: 80%;
      max-width:300px;
      background: #777;
      -webkit-box-shadow: 0 18px 10px #777;
      -moz-box-shadow: 0 18px 10px #777;
      box-shadow: 0 18px 10px #777;
      -webkit-transform: rotate(-4deg);
      -moz-transform: rotate(-4deg);
      -o-transform: rotate(-4deg);
      -ms-transform: rotate(-4deg);
      transform: rotate(-4deg);
    }

    .v-panel:after {
      -webkit-transform: rotate(4deg);
      -moz-transform: rotate(43deg);
      -o-transform: rotate(4deg);
      -ms-transform: rotate(4deg);
```

```
    transform: rotate(4deg);
    right: 10px;
    left: auto;
}
```

A lot of CSS, but it's worth it. Take a look at the cool result:

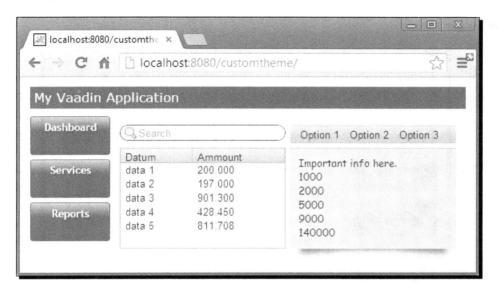

Styling menus

On menus we have `v-menubar` for the menu bar, `v-menubar-menuitem` for the items, and `v-menubar-menuitem-selected` for selected items. Here is an example:

```
.v-menubar {
  color: #fff;
  background: #8495ea;
  border: 1px solid #4455aa;
  text-shadow: 1px 1px 0px #474746;
  border-radius: 10px;
  -webkit-border-radius: 10px;
  -moz-border-radius: 10px;
}

.v-menubar-menuitem {
  background: #8495ea;
}

.v-menubar-menuitem:hover {
```

```
    background-color: #4455aa;
}


.v-menubar-menuitem-selected {
    background-color: #6475ca;
}
```

And we got a brand new menu:

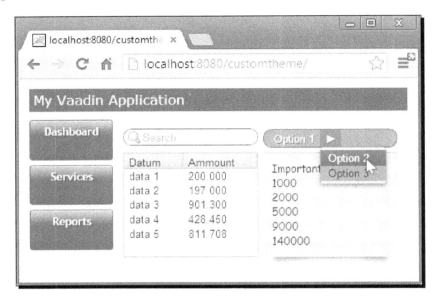

Styling tables

Because tables are big components, they have a lot of classes for every section and element in the tables. Remember that you can always use your browser to inspect the HTML and seek for the CSS classes you need. Here you have a snippet to change the background color, the header color, and add a hover effect on table rows:

```
.v-table-header {
    color: #fff;
    background: #4455aa;
    font-weight: bold;
    text-align: center;
}


.v-table {
    background: #99afff;
```

```
  }

  .v-table-row:hover, .v-table-row-odd:hover {
    color: #fff;
    background: #6475ca;
  }
```

Here is the result:

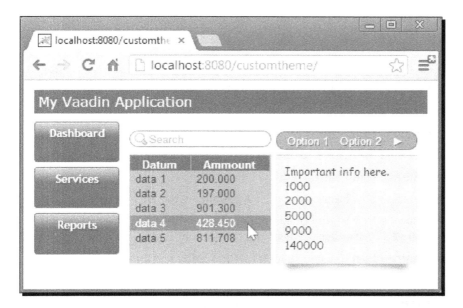

Pop quiz – Vaadin themes

Time to check your knowledge level:

Q1. Vaadin themes are located at:

1. /themes.
2. /VAADIN/themes.
3. /WEB-INF/themes.

Q2. To use the chameleon theme you must use the annotation:

1. @VaadinTheme(BaseTheme.Chameleon).
2. @Theme(BaseTheme.Chameleon).
3. @Theme("chameleon").

Q3. If you inspect an HTML element like `<div class="v-label" style="height: 100%">` ..., and you want to change its background color using CSS, you can do (select two answers):

1. `div { background: #fff; }`.
2. `.div { background: #fff; }`.
3. `v-label { background: #fff; }`.
4. `.v-label { background: #fff; }`.

Summary

We learned some classic, old-school web development stuff in this chapter. Look at what we have covered:

- We met four out-of-the-box Vaadin themes.
- We learned how Vaadin allows us to define our own themes using Sass.
- We learned some basics of CSS.
- We learned how Sass extends CSS by adding variables, nesting, and mixins.
- We learned that Vaadin UI components are rendered as HTML elements with proper CSS classes according to the component's type.
- We learned how to use inspect HTML in Firefox and Chrome.
- We learned how to create a new Vaadin theme.
- We saw several examples of customizing some of the most common Vaadin UI components.

At this point you must be quite proficient with Vaadin. You have used most Vaadin UI components, you know how Vaadin data model works, and you can use some basic CSS and Sass to customize your components and create new themes.

The next chapter is going to be the perfect closure for our Vaadin trip: We'll learn how to develop custom components. See you there!

8

Developing Your Own Components

Standing on the shoulders of giants, Vaadin offers you a variety of UI components on top of GWT, taking all the client/server communication implementation details off you. However, Vaadin doesn't limit you to the included UI components. You have all the GWT power to develop your own!

This chapter will cover the following topics:

- ◆ Custom components
- ◆ Client-side applications and compiling to JavaScript
- ◆ Widgets
- ◆ Remote procedure calls
- ◆ Extensions
- ◆ Custom JavaScript

In this chapter, you will use the **Vaadin client side framework** to compile Java code into JavaScript. You will develop a custom component, a pure client-side application, a client-side component that communicates with server, and a custom JavaScript component sponsored by JQuery. Let's start the last stretch of our journey.

Custom components

The easiest way to create a custom component is by extending some existing component. For example, we can extend `Label` to automatically add some custom styles, and set a default caption shown as follows:

```
class MyFancyLabel extends Label {
  public MyFancyLabel() {
    addStyleName("my-fancy-label");
    setCaption("Fancy default caption");
  }
}
```

Most of the time, we will need a mixture of UI components, so extending a unique component won't work in these situations. `CustomComponent` to the rescue. The previous `MyFancyLabel` could be implemented like this:

```
class MyFancyLabel extends CustomComponent {
  public MyFancyLabel() {
    Label label = new Label("Fancy default caption");
    label.addStyleName("my-fancy-label");
    setCompositionRoot(label);
  }
}
```

`CustomComponent` defines the `setCompositionRoot` method which allows us to define which component will act as the root of our composition. We could create a component hierarchy and then call the `setCompositionRoot` method passing the corresponding root of this hierarchy.

There is another important reason to use `CustomComponent`. `CustomComponent` hides the internal implementation. That way, it is very easy to change the internal implementation of the component without the risk of breaking anything of the code that uses it. It offers a clear cut between the application and the components because it is only accessible through the API that the developer defines.

Enough is enough. No more theory. Let's bring to life a real custom component.

Time for action – creating a custom component

Have you ever accepted license terms when installing software? Sometimes you can click the **Install** button only and only if you have previously checked a **Yeah right. I do Accept the Terms** checkbox. Let's make a custom component to emulate that corporate praised behavior. The steps to create a custom component are as follows:

1. Create a new Vaadin project with the name *customcomponent* using your IDE.

2. Create a new class extending CustomComponent:

    ```
    public class AcceptTermsButton extends CustomComponent {

    }
    ```

3. We need three components: a CheckBox, a Button, and a VerticalLayout:

    ```
    public class AcceptTermsButton extends CustomComponent {

        private VerticalLayout layout = new VerticalLayout();
        private CheckBox checkbox = new CheckBox();
        private Button button = new Button();

    }
    ```

     We are defining the components as class members only to emphasize that we are creating a composition of objects, but actually we only need button to be a class member.

4. Create a constructor to build our custom component up:

    ```
    public class AcceptTermsButton extends CustomComponent {

        //...

        public AcceptTermsButton(String checkboxCaption,
          String buttonCaption) {

            layout.setSpacing(true);

            checkbox.setCaption(checkboxCaption);
            checkbox.addValueChangeListener(new ValueChangeListener() {
              @Override
              public void valueChange(ValueChangeEvent event) {
    ```

```
        button.setEnabled(checkbox.getValue());
      }
    });

    button.setCaption(buttonCaption);
    button.setEnabled(false);

    layout.addComponent(checkbox);
    layout.addComponent(button);

    setCompositionRoot(layout);
  }

}
```

5. We need to allow adding `ClickListener` instances to our internal button:

```
public class AcceptTermsButton extends CustomComponent {

  // ...

  public void addClickListener(ClickListener listener) {
    button.addClickListener(listener);
  }

}
```

6. Our custom component is ready. We can use it exactly the same as we use regular UI components. Here is an example:

```
public class CustomcomponentUI extends UI {

  protected void init(VaadinRequest request) {
    final VerticalLayout layout = new VerticalLayout();
    layout.setMargin(true);
    setContent(layout);

    Label terms = new Label(
        "You agree with us on everything.");

    Panel panel = new Panel("LICENSE TERMS:");
    panel.setContent(terms);
```

```
        layout.addComponent(panel);

        AcceptTermsButton button = new AcceptTermsButton(
            "Yeah right. I do accept that.", "Install");

        button.addClickListener(new ClickListener() {
          @Override
          public void buttonClick(ClickEvent event) {
            Notification.show("Software installed.");
          }
        });

        layout.addComponent(button);
    }
}
```

7. That's it. You can run the application now.

What just happened?

We have created a custom component by using object oriented composition. The `AcceptTerms` constructor sets up a layout containing the needed `CheckBox` and `Button` components. Once the components tree thrives, we announce who is going to be the root of all evil, I mean, the root of our custom component:

```
setCompositionRoot(layout);
```

The screenshot of the application is as follows:

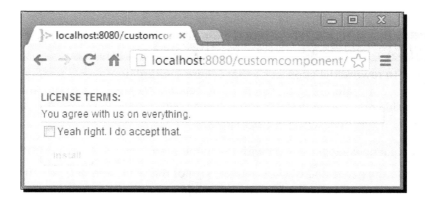

Something cool about `CustomComponent` is that you can use the **Vaadin Visual Editor** in Eclipse to visually design your components. If you like drag-and-drop to design user interfaces, you're going to love it. We are not explaining too much about Vaadin Visual Editor here, except that it is cool, easy to use, and will generate `CustomComponent` code for you. For more information visit `http://dev.vaadin.com/wiki/Addons/VisualEditor`.

Client side applications

We have seen how to create a composition of server-side UI components. This approach is good if you can rely on existing components. But, what if you need something new? What if you need a high responsive component that avoids going to the server too frequently? What if you need some fine-grained tuning on some UI component? The Vaadin client side framework is the tool to accomplish this kind of requirements.

Vaadin client framework is based on GWT, so everything you can do with GWT, you can do with Vaadin. In this section we are going to develop a pure client side application using the Vaadin client side framework.

 Explaining GWT would require a whole book. In fact, there are some really good books on the matter such as *Google Web Toolkit 2 Application Development Cookbook* by *S. Ahammad* and *Google App Engine Java and GWT Application Development* by *D. Guermeur and A. Unruh*. For our purposes, we are going to learn some fundamental aspects of GWT, but remember that this is only the tip of the iceberg.

Time for action – creating a client side application

We are going to rewrite the application that Eclipse's wizard or Maven's archetype, depending on your preferred tool, generates by default. We are going to turn it into a pure client side application that you can use even without a web server. The steps to create a client side application are as follows:

1. Create a new Vaadin project with the name *clientsideapp* using your IDE.
2. Delete the generated UI class and any sign of the UI class in `web.xml` (that is, the `server` and `server-mapping` elements).

3. Create a new entry point class for our application, please make sure you put your classes in the correct package (don't omit the `.client` part of the package as GWT expects this class to be in a package like this by convention):

```
package clientsideapp.client;

public class MyEntryPoint {

}
```

4. Let this class implement `com.google.gwt.core.client.EntryPoint`:

```
public class MyEntryPoint implements EntryPoint {

    @Override
    public void onModuleLoad() {
    }

}
```

5. Implement the UI logic using standard GWT components instead of Vaadin components (make sure your imports match the listed packages):

```
import com.google.gwt.core.client.EntryPoint;
import com.google.gwt.event.dom.client.ClickEvent;
import com.google.gwt.event.dom.client.ClickHandler;
import com.google.gwt.user.client.ui.Button;
import com.google.gwt.user.client.ui.Label;
import com.google.gwt.user.client.ui.RootPanel;

public class MyEntryPoint implements EntryPoint {

    @Override
    public void onModuleLoad() {
        Button button = new Button("Click Me");
        button.addClickHandler(new ClickHandler() {
            @Override
            public void onClick(ClickEvent event) {
                RootPanel.get().add(new Label("Thank you for
                    clicking"));
            }
        });
        RootPanel.get().add(button);
    }

}
```

6. Now we need to include **module descriptor** which contains instructions for the Vaadin client compiler. Add a new XML file with the name `ClientsideappWidgetset.gwt.xml` in the *clientsideapp* package. Make sure the content of the file matches6 the following:

```xml
<?xml version="1.0" encoding="UTF-8"?>
<!DOCTYPE module PUBLIC "-//Google Inc.//DTD Google Web Toolkit
1.7.0//EN" "http://google-web-toolkit.googlecode.com/svn/
tags/1.7.0/distro-source/core/src/gwt-module.dtd">
<module>
  <inherits name="com.vaadin.Vaadin" />

    <entry-point class="clientsideapp.client.MyEntryPoint"/>
</module>
```

7. Make sure your files are arranged shown as follows before proceeding:

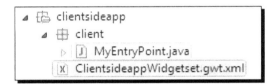

 Why is the author being so sensitive about file location and content? Vaadin client side framework is an advanced topic we had never faced before. We have to be careful about how we take each step.

8. We can compile to JavaScript now.

❑ If you are using Eclipse, click on the **Compile Vaadin widgets** button on the toolbar:

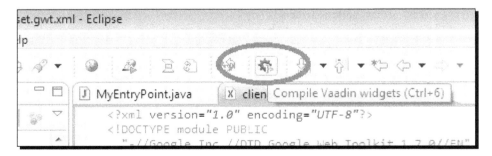

❑ If you are using NetBeans or Maven, run the `vaadin:compile` goal. For example, in the terminal move to your project location and run:

```
mvn vaadin:compile
```

If everything went right, you will see a **Compilation succeeded** message.

9. We have our JavaScript ready. All we need to do now is to create an HTML page that includes the generated JavaScript. Create a simple HTML file (`index.html`) to call the compiled JavaScript:

```html
<!doctype html>
<html>
  <head>
    <meta http-equiv="content-type" content=
      "text/html; charset=UTF-8">
    <title>Client Side Application Test</title>
    <script type="text/javascript" src= "???" >
    </script>
  </head>
  <body>
  </body>
</html>
```

10. Where is the JavaScript Vaadin client compiler generated? We need that information to change that useless `???` in the script element of the previous snippet. So, where is it? Well, the answer is... in the `VAADIN/widgetsets` directory:

The highlighted file is the script we have to call in our HTML file. So, replace `???` with `VAADIN/widgetsets/clientsideapp.ClientsideappWidgetset/clientsideapp.ClientsideappWidgetset.nocache.js`. What a long path!

11. Execute the application as usual by deploying and starting your preferred server, just for now.

What just happened?

Let's quickly review what we have done. We created a new Vaadin application and deleted any class, servlet, and servlet mapping. Then, we created a GWT `EntryPoint` class to define all the UI logic using standard GWT components. Next, we defined a GWT module descriptor to allow the Vaadin client compiler do its job. We compiled the Java class using the Vaadin client compiler. The generated JavaScript was placed somewhere inside the `VAADIN/widgetsets` directory. Finally, we took this JavaScript (`clientsideapp.ClientsideappWidgetset.nocache.js`) and created an HTML file calling it.

This is a screenshot of the application:

This application is now running independently in the browser. It doesn't need any further server connectivity.

Have a go hero – check that the app is purely client side

Shut the server down (but don't close your browser!) and click on the **Click Me** button a couple of times. The application must keep showing thankful messages. Get rid of the server. Copy all the generated files to an external directory in your hard drive along with the HTML file we created, and open the HTML file directly in your browser. Make sure your `script` element points to the generated JavaScript file.

We have intentionally omitted a lot of explanation about the usage of GWT components and GWT module descriptors. The aim of the previous example was only to introduce you to the GWT world and show you how the Vaadin client compiler generates JavaScript from Java classes. For more information on GWT, visit `https://developers.google.com/web-toolkit`.

Widgets

You might think:

Reader: Cool! Vaadin can compile Java classes into JavaScript. But we didn't make any compilation of this kind in the previous chapters, and we created several applications.

Author: Well, in previous chapters we were using only **server components**.

Reader: Server what?

Author: Server components, or simply components, such as `Label`, `Button`, and others, they are Java classes which are not compiled into JavaScript.

Reader: That's obvious; we didn't make any compilation to JavaScript.

Author: That's right. Vaadin team performed the compilation for us and packaged the generated "widget set" inside one of the jars we are using.

Reader: Wait! What is a **widget set**?

Author: Oh, I'm sorry. I'm kind of a messy teacher. Well, what you see on the pages in your browser are **widgets**. A widget is like a piece of JavaScript that was generated by the Vaadin client compiler. A widget set, is then a collection of several widgets. At the end, the widget set is what the Vaadin client compiler produces.

Reader: I understand. So, if a widget is generated by the Vaadin client compiler, it means that the widget comes from a Java class, right?

Author: Totally!

Reader: But wait. `Label` is a (server) component because I've been using it in my projects, and I didn't have to compile any widget set. I can really see labels in my pages, so those labels are widgets. But the `Label` class is not the one that is being compiled to JavaScript because, as you said before, `Label` is a (server) component. So, there must be another class.

Author: Exactly, `Label` is a server component and it is not being compiled by the Vaadin client compiler. The one that is being compiled is `com.vaadin.client.ui.VLabel`. So, `VLabel` is a widget and `Label` is a (server) component. They both communicate through a `Connector` object. A `Connector` object is a place where you can code all the client-server communication logic. But let me explain all this to you with an example.

Reader: Yes, please!

Time for action – creating a widget

We are going to develop a custom widget to show a marquee. Follow these steps to create
your first widget:

1. Create a new Vaadin project with the name *myfistwidget* using your IDE.

2. Create a new class for the client side widget `myfirstwidget.client.`
   `MarqueeLabelWidget`:

```
package myfirstwidget.client;

import com.google.gwt.dom.client.Style.Position;
import com.google.gwt.dom.client.Style.Unit;
import com.google.gwt.user.client.Element;
import com.google.gwt.user.client.Timer;
import com.google.gwt.user.client.ui.Label;

public class MarqueeLabelWidget extends Label {

// ...

  public MarqueeLabelWidget() {
    final Element element = getElement();
    element.getStyle().setPosition(Position.RELATIVE);

    Timer timer = new Timer() {
      private int left = 0;

      @Override
      public void run() {
        element.getStyle().setLeft(left, Unit.PX);
        left++;
      }
    };

    timer.scheduleRepeating(100);
  }
}
```

3. Create a new `myfirstwidget.client.MarqueeLabelState` class to store the component state:

```
package myfirstwidget.client;
import com.vaadin.shared.AbstractComponentState;

public class MarqueeLabelState extends AbstractComponentState {

  public String text = "";

}
```

4. Create a new class for the server-side component `myfirstwidget.MarqueeLabel` (note that the package does not contain `.client`):

```
package myfirstwidget;

import myfirstwidget.client.MarqueeLabelState;

import com.vaadin.ui.AbstractComponent;

public class MarqueeLabel extends AbstractComponent {

  @Override
  public MarqueeLabelState getState() {
    return (MarqueeLabelState) super.getState();
  }

  @Override
  public void setCaption(String caption) {
    getState().text = caption;
  }

}
```

5. Create a new class to connect the widget with the server side component `myfirstwidget.client.MarqueeLabelConnector`:

```
package myfirstwidget.client;

import myfirstwidget.MarqueeLabel;

import com.google.gwt.core.shared.GWT;
import com.google.gwt.user.client.ui.Widget;
import com.vaadin.client.communication.StateChangeEvent;
```

```
import com.vaadin.client.ui.AbstractComponentConnector;
import com.vaadin.shared.ui.Connect;

@Connect(MarqueeLabel.class)
public class MarqueeLabelConnector extends
AbstractComponentConnector {

  @Override
  public Widget createWidget() {
    return GWT.create(MarqueeLabelWidget.class);
  }

  @Override
  public MarqueeLabelWidget getWidget() {
    return (MarqueeLabelWidget) super.getWidget();
  }

  @Override
  public MarqueeLabelState getState() {
    return (MarqueeLabelState) super.getState();
  }

  @Override
  public void onStateChanged(StateChangeEvent stateChangeEvent) {
    super.onStateChanged(stateChangeEvent);
    getWidget().setText(getState().text);
  }

}
```

6. Create the module descriptor `MyfirstwidgetWidgetset.gwt.xml` inside the `myfirstwidget` **package:**

```
<?xml version="1.0" encoding="UTF-8"?>
<!DOCTYPE module PUBLIC "-//Google Inc.//DTD Google Web Toolkit
  1.7.0//EN" "http://google-web-
  toolkit.googlecode.com/svn/tags/1.7.0/distro-
  source/core/src/gwt-module.dtd">
<module>
    <inherits name="com.vaadin.DefaultWidgetSet" />
</module>
```

7. Modify your UI class to use the new component:

```
public class MyfirstwidgetUI extends UI {

  @Override
  protected void init(VaadinRequest request) {
    final VerticalLayout layout = new VerticalLayout();
    layout.setMargin(true);
    setContent(layout);

    MarqueeLabel marquee = new MarqueeLabel();
    marquee.setCaption("Hello Custom Widget!");
    layout.addComponent(marquee);
  }

}
```

8. Compile the widgets by clicking on **Compile Vaadin widgets** in Eclipse or running the vaadin:compile **Maven goal.**

9. Add your widget set as a parameter of the Vaadin servlet in web.xml:

```
<web-app ...>

  ...
  <servlet>

  ...
    <init-param>
      <description>Application widgetset</description>
      <param-name>widgetset</param-name>
      <param-value>myfirstwidget.MyfirstwidgetWidgetset
        </param-value>
    </init-param>

  </servlet>

  ...

</web-app>
```

10. Run the application.

What just happened?

You have created your first widget with server-side connectivity. Let's see how it works.

We created a package `myfirstwidget.client`. This package contains all the Java classes for the Vaadin client compiler. The first class we implemented was `MarqueeLabelWidget` that extends the GWT `Label` class:

```
public class MarqueeLabelWidget extends Label {
  // ...
}
```

Inside the constructor, we used the `getElement` method to get a reference to the actual HTML element that constitutes the widget. Then we used the awesome GWT API to modify the element. Specifically, the `left` CSS attribute of the element, which establishes the amount of space from the left of the element. In this example we used a `Timer`, to schedule our logic at certain time, so that we can animate the label.

Next, we created a new separate class to store the state of the component. We just needed a `String` to keep the text to be shown in the `marquee` element:

```
public class MarqueeLabelState extends AbstractComponentState {

  public String text = "";

}
```

We extended `AbstractComponentState` which is the default implementation for `AbstractComponent`. Our server side component extends `AbstractComponent` as shown in the following code snippet:

```
public class MarqueeLabel extends AbstractComponent {

  @Override
  public MarqueeLabelState getState() { ... }

  @Override
  public void setCaption(String caption) { ... }

}
```

MarqueeLabel is the server component that we can add to our Vaadin layouts. Note that the setCaption method doesn't deal directly with any MarqueeLabelWidget method; it just changes the current state of the component. When the state changes the MarqueeLabelConnector.onStateChanged method will be called. Take a look at the connector as shown in the following code:

```
@Connect(MarqueeLabel.class)
public class MarqueeLabelConnector extends AbstractComponentConnector
{

  public Widget createWidget() {
    return GWT.create(MarqueeLabelWidget.class);
  }

  @Override
  public MarqueeLabelWidget getWidget() { ... }

  @Override
  public MarqueeLabelState getState() { ... }

  @Override
  public void onStateChanged(StateChangeEvent stateChangeEvent) {
    super.onStateChanged(stateChangeEvent);
    getWidget().setText(getState().text);
  }

}
```

First of all, we annotated the class with @Connect(MarqueeLabel.class). This means that the connector is connecting a client side widget to the concrete server component MarqueeLabel. On the other hand, the createWidget method connects to MarqueeLabelWidget by creating an instance with the help of GWT.

 We have to use the GWT.create method to allow *deferred binding* when compiling widget sets. To make a long story short, deferred binding is used to generate the JavaScript for each specific browser such as Firefox or Chrome. You can read the long story at https://developers.google.com/web-toolkit/doc/latest/DevGuideCodingBasicsDeferred.

We also need to extend getWidget to return our specific widget class, and getState to return our specific state class.

Finally, we defined a module descriptor that inherits the default Vaadin widget set (courtesy of Vaadin team). Note that we didn't define an entry point here because we are not creating a pure client-side application.

Remote procedure calls

Are you wondering how a widget can send a message to the related server component? If you have been curious, you might have noticed an addClickHandler method that you can use in your widget. That method seems to be appropriate. The problem is that by using this method you have to implement the click logic in the widget, which means that the click event will be handled in the client.

Remote Procedure Calls (RPC) will solve the problem. RPC are made through an interface that extends Vaadin's ServerRpc. For example:

```
public interface MarqueeLabelServerRpc extends ServerRpc {

  public void clicked();

}
```

 ServerRpc is used for communication from client to server. You have to extend ClientRpc if your communication is going from server to client though.

The previous interface declares a method that can be called from the client side. Normally, the call will be done from the connector (it makes sense to implement a connection feature in the connector, right?). To make the call we need an instance of MarqueeLabelServerRpc. We create the instance with the help of RpcProxy as shown in the following code snippet:

```
public class MarqueeLabelConnector extends AbstractComponentConnector
{

  private MarqueeLabelServerRpc rpc = RpcProxy.create(
    MarqueeLabelServerRpc.class, this);

  // ...

}
```

Now we can add a ClickHandler (that will be called in the client side), and delegate to the server the click logic by using the rpc object:

```
public class MarqueeLabelConnector extends AbstractComponentConnector
{

  private MarqueeLabelServerRpc rpc = RpcProxy.create(
```

```
        MarqueeLabelServerRpc.class, this);

    public MarqueeLabelConnector() {
        getWidget().addClickHandler(new ClickHandler() {
            @Override
            public void onClick(ClickEvent event) {
                rpc.clicked(); // server's call
            }
        });
    }

    // ...

}
```

The server can accept this call by registering an instance of our RPC interface:

```
public class MarqueeLabel extends AbstractComponent {

    public MarqueeLabel() {
        registerRpc(new MarqueeLabelServerRpc() {
            @Override
            public void clicked() {
                Notification
                    .show("You clicked, so I made an RPC to the server.");
            }
        });
    }

    // ...

}
```

Extensions

In *Chapter 6, Adding More Components* we used the `FileDownloader` extension to add downloading capabilities to a button:

```
// create an extension
FileDownloader downloader = new FileDownloader(resource);

// extend a component
downloader.extend(button);
```

Extensions allow us to add functionality at runtime. We can add multiple extensions to the same component, that's something we cannot do by extending a class (in the object oriented sense, of course).

Time for action – creating an extension

The steps for creating an extension to hide a label when the mouse pointer moves over it are as follows:

1. Create a new Vaadin project with the name **extension** using your IDE.

2. Create a new server-side extension class:

```
public class HideOnHover extends AbstractExtension {

  public void extend(Label label) {
    super.extend(label);
  }

}
```

3. Create a new client side connector (remember to put this class inside a .client package):

```
@Connect(HideOnHover.class)
public class HideOnHoverConnector extends
  AbstractExtensionConnector {

  @Override
  protected void extend(ServerConnector target) {
    final Widget widget = ((ComponentConnector)
      target).getWidget();

    widget.addHandler(new MouseOverHandler() {
      @Override
      public void onMouseOver(MouseOverEvent event) {
        widget.setVisible(false);
      }
    }, MouseOverEvent.getType());
  }

}
```

4. Use the extension in your UI class:

```
Label textField = new Label(
    "Do you dare to put the cursor over me?");
layout.addComponent(textField);

HideOnHover extension = new HideOnHover();
extension.extend(textField);
```

5. Create a module descriptor similar to the one presented in the previous example.

6. Compile the widgets, run the application, and accept the challenge.

What just happened?

We created an extension by implementing two classes. A server-side `AbstractExtension` and its client side counterpart `AbstractExtensionConnector`. The `HideOnHover` extension defines the `extend` method accepting a `Label`. This parameter defines the type of components that can be extended. On the client side, `HideOnHoverConnector` uses the GWT API to add `MouseOverHandler` that detects when the mouse cursor moves over the widget in order to hide it.

Have a go hero – experiment with GWT handlers

Try experimenting with other handlers. GWT comes with plenty of them. Take a look at the GWT documentation at `https://developers.google.com/web-toolkit` and search for the `EventHandler` hierarchy API.

Custom JavaScript

Vaadin is really JavaScript friendly. You can call JavaScript from the server, create JavaScript components and JavaScript extensions not to mention GWT capabilities such as JavaScript native interface and JavaScript overlay types.

 For more information on GWT JavaScript integration, visit `https://developers.google.com/web-toolkit`.

Calling JavaScript from the server

Calling JavaScript from the server is as easy as this:

```
JavaScript.getCurrent().execute("alert('Hello from server side.')");
```

That's it.

Calling the server from JavaScript

We can call our server from the client side using JavaScript. We need to add a JavaScript function as shown in the following code snippet:

```
JavaScript.getCurrent().addFunction("myFunction",
    new JavaScriptFunction() {
        @Override
        public void call(JSONArray arguments) throws JSONException {
            Notification
                .show("JavaScript called me, I show this message.");
        }
    });
```

Now client side JavaScript can make a regular call to `myFunction`. If we are running our application in the browser, we could just type `javascript:window.myFunction()` in the browser's URL bar to show the notification:

JavaScript components

JavaScript's world is big. There are tons of ready-to-use components out there. For example, take a look at the spinner component at `http://jqueryui.com/spinner`. Go ahead and take a look at it. It's a nice component to introduce an integer value by clicking on some little up and down arrows:

If you have a boss, she might say "We've got to put that in our application right now!". Don't be scared. Remember that Vaadin is JavaScript friendly. You will be surprised at how easy it is to incorporate a JavaScript component into Vaadin applications.

Time for action – creating a JavaScript component

Follow these steps and see how easy is to incorporate an existing JavaScript component in Vaadin applications:

1. Create a new Vaadin project with the name *javascriptspinner* using your IDE.

2. Create a new class for our custom JavaScript based component inside a `javascriptspinner` package:

```
@JavaScript({ "spinner.js",
    "http://code.jquery.com/jquery-1.9.1.js",
    "http://code.jquery.com/ui/1.10.3/jquery-ui.js" })
public class Spinner extends AbstractJavaScriptComponent {
}
```

3. Place a new JavaScript file `spinner.js` beside the previous class:

```
javascriptspinner_Spinner = function() {
  var e = this.getElement();
  e.innerHTML = "<input id='spinner' />";
  var spinner = $("#spinner").spinner();
};
```

4. Use the component as you would with any other Vaadin UI component:

```
public class JavascriptspinnerUI extends UI {

  protected void init(VaadinRequest request) {
    final VerticalLayout layout = new VerticalLayout();
    layout.setMargin(true);
    setContent(layout);

    Spinner spinner = new Spinner();
    layout.addComponent(spinner);
  }

}
```

5. No need to compile widgets. Just run your application.

What just happened?

Was that easy? It was! Take a look at our new UI component:

Cool isn't it?

We created a new `Spinner` class extending `AbstractJavaScriptComponent`. This is our custom JavaScript UI component. We annotated the class with `@JavaScript`. This annotation allows us to include the JavaScript files that Vaadin will use to seek the JavaScript code in order to render our spinner component. We are including three:

- `http://code.jquery.com/jquery-1.9.1.js`
- `http://code.jquery.com/ui/1.10.3/jquery-ui.js`
- `spinner.js`

The first two are external files that we require to use the nice spinner from **jQuery UI**.

 jQuery and **jQuery UI** are JavaScript libraries. jQuery makes things like HTML document traversal and manipulation, event handling, animation, and Ajax much simpler with an easy-to-use API that works across a multitude of browsers. jQuery UI is a set of user interface interactions, effects, widgets, and themes built on top of jQuery. You can find more information about these libraries at `http://jquery.com` and `http://jqueryui.com`.

The `spinner.js` file contains our own JavaScript code. How does Vaadin know which JavaScript function to call? Simple: Using a naming convention. Our JavaScript component's full class name is `javascriptspinner.Spinner`. Vaadin will replace dots with underscores, so `javascriptspinner.Spinner` becomes `javascriptspinner_Spinner`. That's exactly the name of the JavaScript function Vaadin will call when our component is attached. The function must be located in any of the files we specified in the `@JavaScript` annotation. The `javascriptspinner_Spinner` function just takes the current HTML element, replaces its inner HTML code, and calls the proper spinner function of jQuery UI.

You can use states and RPC similar to what we did with the widgets.

JavaScript extensions

You can develop Vaadin extensions based on JavaScript. For example, let's say we want to add some cool jQuery effect. First, we need extend `AbstractJavaScriptExtension`:

```
@JavaScript({ "cooleffect.js",
    "http://code.jquery.com/jquery-1.9.1.js" })
public class CoolEffect extends AbstractJavaScriptExtension {

    public void extend(AbstractClientConnector component) {
        super.extend(component);
    }

}
```

Then, we have to implement a `javascriptextension_CoolEffect` JavaScript function. We have added `cooleffect.js` in our `@JavaScript` annotation, so we implement the function right there:

```
javascriptextension_CoolEffect = function() {
    // get the connector
    var connectorId = this.getParentId();
    // get the HTML element to animate (the widget)
    var element = this.getElement(connectorId);

    $(element).animate({marginTop: '80px', opacity: 0.0}, 0);
    $(element).animate({marginTop: '0px', opacity: 1.0}, 900);
};
```

This method basically moves the widget to an initial position and then runs a nice animation. That's all. Now we can use the extension as usual. For example:

```
CoolEffect effect = new CoolEffect();
effect.extend(panel);
```

Have a go hero – implement a JavaScript extension

Try implementing the previous extension. Use any jQuery effect you like. If you want to see the extension in action, take a look at the *javascriptextension* example.

Pop quiz – CustomComponents

It's time to check our knowledge level:

Q1. `CustomComponent` allows you to create a client side component:

1. That's absolutely true.
2. That's not true.

Q2. Vaadin client side compiler:

1. Compiles JavaScript to generate widget sets.
2. Takes a widget set and generates JavaScript and CSS.
3. Compiles Java into widget sets in JavaScript.

Q3. To develop a custom client side component that communicates with the server, you can use the classes or interfaces:

1. `ClientSideComponent`, `AbstractComponent`.
2. `ClientSideComponent`, `AbstractComponent`, Connector.
3. Widget, `AbstractComponent`, Connector.

Q4. When you create a `JavaScriptExtension`, you must compile the widgets:

1. That's absolutely true.
2. That's not true.

Summary

We've learned some key aspects of Vaadin client side development. Take a look at the cool things we did:

- ◆ We learned how to implement custom components using object-oriented composition.

- ◆ We saw that Java is compiled into JavaScript by the Vaadin client side compiler.

- ◆ We learned that a Widget is a client side component and the Vaadin client side compiler generates it as JavaScript.

- ◆ We learned that a Widget can be paired with a server side UI component by implementing a `Connector` interface annotated with `@Connect`.

- ◆ We learned how to make remote procedure calls from a client-side widget to a server-side component.

- ◆ We learned how to implement Vaadin extensions by extending `AbstractExtension`.

- ◆ We learned how to call JavaScript from the server and how to call the server from JavaScript.

- ◆ We learned how to implement JavaScript extensions by extending `AbstractJavaScriptExtension` and annotating the class with `@JavaScript`.

It was an awesome trip! We didn't see every aspect of Vaadin; but we now are able to develop a huge range of cool RIA applications using Vaadin. Hope you found developing web applications with Vaadin as satisfying as I did. Cheers!

Pop Quiz Answers

Chapter 1, Writing Your First Vaadin-powered Application

Pop quiz – Vaadin fundamentals

Q1	2
Q2	3

Chapter 2, Using Input Components and Forms – Time to Listen to Users

Pop quiz – thinking in Vaadin

Q1	3
Q2	1
Q3	3
Q4	2
Q5	3
Q6	1

Chapter 3, Arranging Components into Layouts

Pop quiz – mastering layouts

Q1	6
Q2	3
Q3	2
Q4	3
Q5	2

Chapter 4, Using Vaadin Navigation Capabilities

Pop quiz – navigation capabilities

Q1	3
Q2	3
Q3	1 and 3
Q4	2
Q5	2

Chapter 5, Using Tables – Time to Talk to Users

Pop quiz – mastering tables

Q1	3
Q2	3
Q3	1
Q4	3
Q5	2
Q6	1
Q7	4

Chapter 6, Adding More Components

Pop quiz – more components

Q1	1
Q2	3
Q3	3
Q4	3
Q5	3
Q6	2

Chapter 7, Customizing UI Components – Time to Theme it

Pop quiz – Vaadin themes

Q1	2
Q2	3
Q3	1 and 4

Chapter 8, Developing Your Own Components

Pop quiz – custom components

Q1	2
Q2	3
Q3	3
Q4	2

Index

GWT.create method 207
GWT handlers 211

H

HeaderClickLister method 121
headers
  about 120, 121
  clicking on 121
hello world application 23
HIDDEN, enum value 120
HTML
  inspecting 178

I

icon property 47
icons
  about 154
  adding, steps for 154, 155
ID, enum value 120
Image class 158
immediate mode 38
initCombo method 38
init method 54
InlineDateField component
  using 59
input components
  about 52
  adding, in layout 41
  value, getting 37
  value, setting 37
int object type 30
ItemClickEvent method 127
ItemClickListener method 127
items
  about 51
  in tables, selecting 126
Ivy 10
IvyDE 10

J

JavaScript
  about 211
  calling, from server 211, 212
  components 212
  components, creating 213

extensions 215
extensions, implementing 215
java.util.Date object 58
jQuery 214
jQuery UI 214

K

Kind of option 55

L

Label component 50
labels
  about 19, 21
  styling 181
layout
  about 48, 64
  main layout 64-66
  margin 22, 23
  size, setting 68
lowerSection component 67

M

MarqueeLabelConnector.onStateChanged
    method 207
MarqueeLabelWidget method 207
Maven
  Vaadin application, creating 15
  Vaadin application, deploying 17
  Vaadin application, running 15-17
menus
  about 106-108
  icons, adding to menu items 108
  options, adding 72, 73
  styling 187, 188
MethodProperty instance 132
Mixins 177
module descriptor 198

N

navigators
  about 98
  programmatically 100-103
  using 98, 99
nesting 176

Thank you for buying
Vaadin 7 UI Design By Example Beginner's Guide

About Packt Publishing

Packt, pronounced 'packed', published its first book "*Mastering phpMyAdmin for Effective MySQL Management*" in April 2004 and subsequently continued to specialize in publishing highly focused books on specific technologies and solutions.

Our books and publications share the experiences of your fellow IT professionals in adapting and customizing today's systems, applications, and frameworks. Our solution based books give you the knowledge and power to customize the software and technologies you're using to get the job done. Packt books are more specific and less general than the IT books you have seen in the past. Our unique business model allows us to bring you more focused information, giving you more of what you need to know, and less of what you don't.

Packt is a modern, yet unique publishing company, which focuses on producing quality, cutting-edge books for communities of developers, administrators, and newbies alike. For more information, please visit our website: www.packtpub.com.

About Packt Open Source

In 2010, Packt launched two new brands, Packt Open Source and Packt Enterprise, in order to continue its focus on specialization. This book is part of the Packt Open Source brand, home to books published on software built around Open Source licences, and offering information to anybody from advanced developers to budding web designers. The Open Source brand also runs Packt's Open Source Royalty Scheme, by which Packt gives a royalty to each Open Source project about whose software a book is sold.

Writing for Packt

We welcome all inquiries from people who are interested in authoring. Book proposals should be sent to author@packtpub.com. If your book idea is still at an early stage and you would like to discuss it first before writing a formal book proposal, contact us; one of our commissioning editors will get in touch with you.

We're not just looking for published authors; if you have strong technical skills but no writing experience, our experienced editors can help you develop a writing career, or simply get some additional reward for your expertise.

Vaadin 7 Cookbook

ISBN: 978-1-84951-880-2   Paperback: 404 pages

Over 90 recipes for creating Rich Internet Applications with the latest version of Vaadin

1. Covers exciting features such as using drag and n anddrop, creating charts, custom components, lazy loading, server-push functionality, and more

2. Tips for facilitating the development and testing of Vaadin applications

3. Enhance your applications with Spring, Grails, or Roo integration

Learning Vaadin

ISBN: 978-1-84951-522-1   Paperback: 412 pages

Master the full range of web development features powered by Vaadin built RIAs

1. Discover the Vaadin framework in a progressive and structured way

2. Learn about components, events, layouts, containers, and bindings

3. Create outstanding new components by yourself

4. Integrate with your existing frameworks and infrastructure

5. Pragmatic and no-nonsense approach

Please check **www.PacktPub.com** for information on our titles

Ext JS 4 Web Application Development Cookbook

ISBN: 978-1-84951-686-0   Paperback: 488 pages

Over 110 easy-to-follow recipes backed up with real-life examples, walking you through basic Ext JS features to advanced application design using Sencha's Ext JS

1. Learn how to build Rich Internet Applications with the latest version of the Ext JS framework in a cookbook style

2. From creating forms to theming your interface, you will learn the building blocks for developing the perfect web application

3. Easy to follow recipes step through practical and detailed examples which are all fully backed up with code, illustrations, and tips

Web Application Development with Yii and PHP

ISBN: 978-1-84951-872-7   Paperback: 332 pages

Learn the Yii application development framework by taking a step-by-step approach to building a Web-based project task tracking system from conception through production deployment

1. A step-by-step guide to creating a modern Web application using PHP, MySQL, and Yii

2. Build a real-world, user-based, database-driven project task management application using the Yii development framework

3. Start with a general idea, and finish with deploying to production, learning everything about Yii inbetween, from "A"ctive record to "Z"ii component library

Please check **www.PacktPub.com** for information on our titles

www.ingramcontent.com/pod-product-compliance
Lightning Source LLC
Chambersburg PA
CBHW082117070326
40690CB00049B/3594